I0832896

Preterism: Orthodox or Unorthodox?

Jay E. Adams

Institute for Nouthetic Studies, a ministry of Mid-America Baptist Theological Seminary, 5640 Airline Road, Arlington, TN 38002
mabts.edu and nouthetic.org

ISBN: 978-1-970445-31-2 (Print)
ISBN: 978-1-970445-32-9 (eBook)
Old ISBN: 889032-44-1

Editor: Donn R. Arms

Library of Congress Cataloging-in-Publication Data
Names: Adams, Jay E., 1929 - 2020
Title: *Preterism: Orthodox or Unorthodox?*
by Jay E. Adams
Description: Arlington, TN: Institute for Nouthetic Studies, 2026
Identifiers: ISBN 9781970445312 (paper)
Classification: LCC BT824.5 A33 | DDC 223.09

Published in the United States of America

Contents

Introduction:

Preterism vs. Preterism

For some time, writers like Ken Gentry, R. C. Sproul, and myself have taught a view of eschatology (doctrine of the last things) that—for want of a better term—has been labeled "Preterism." The word comes from the Latin *praeteritus* ("to go by, pass"), which, in turn, is based upon *praeter* ("that which is beyond, past"). A Preterist, then, is one who deals with the past. The immediate concern of all Preterists is the prophetic materials found in the Bible. Much of what Futurists believe to be yet unfulfilled, the Preterist sees as already fulfilled in apostolic times. But recently, an old error has been revived that sharply divides the Preterists into two distinct groups—not to be confused. This error is now propagated by a spate of books, conferences, and debates. It is a form of Preterism that denies that there are *any* prophecies yet to be fulfilled, including the Second Coming of Jesus Christ, the resurrection of the body, and the final judgment.

"Ah!" you say. "That proves the preterist view in all of its forms, including yours, is wrong. If it could lead to such denials, then it cannot be correct and must be rejected."

That, of course, is an unfair conclusion. It is like saying, "Fido is a black dog. Therefore, all dogs are black." Indeed, the accusation that all forms of Preterism are wrong because some Preterists are only backfires on those who hold other prophetic viewpoints. Let me remind you that more cultists (including Mormons, Jehovah's Witnesses, and Seventh Day Adventists) espouse premillennial views of the future than any other. That does not make all Premillennialists cultic! It would be quite improper to argue any such thing. The liberals, historically, adopted Postmillennial viewpoints, but that doesn't mean all Postmillennialists are liberals. Again, it would be wrong to make such a claim. To do so, would be to call staunch conservative B. B. Warfield a liberal!

Like those—orthodox and unorthodox—who hold to other prophetic views, there are Preterists and there are Preterists. I prefer to distinguish between those who have been termed "Partial Preterists" and "Full Preterists" as "Orthodox Preterists" and "Unorthodox Preterists." Just as there are cultic Premillennialists and liberal Postmillennialists, so too, there are those who hold to wrong forms of Preterism. This fact, by no means, implies that all Preterists are unsound. As a matter of fact, in this book I shall attempt to expose and refute Unorthodox (or "heretical") Preterism while setting forth something of the Orthodox Preterist teaching. I trust that, whatever your views, you will see clearly that it is not right to lump together and tag the two forms of Preterism with the same label. And, it is my hope that you will come to understand and believe the teachings of Orthodox Preterism as biblical.

1

The Problem

At the outset, let me introduce you to some of the unorthodox views of those who call themselves "full" or "consistent" Preterists. I am doing this up front so that you will be able to understand from their own writings exactly what the problem with this viewpoint is. But I hope that, having read their statements, you will not decide to simply close the book and dismiss Preterism altogether. These Preterists have much to say that is correct. They have opened up an area of thought that, for many, had been rather tightly closed. If they do nothing else, they pose a challenge to beliefs that for years have been uncritically accepted as true by large numbers of Christians in this country. That was not always so. But since the advent of Plymouth Brethren-Scofield Premillennialism, there has been a widespread belief in the idea that many (if not most) of the Old and New Testament prophetic passages pertain to days yet to come. It is that belief which the Preterists have attacked with much vigor (and some success).

Now, the Unorthodox Preterists[1] are not unorthodox in every way—I want to make that clear at the outset. Indeed, some of what they have written is true, useful, and conforms

1 For the sake of saving space, I shall frequently refer to Unorthodox Preterists as UPs and Orthodox Preterists as OPs.

rather closely to the beliefs of Orthodox Preterists. But the UPs go too far. The preterist movement that is now emerging has gained ground because, in the recent past, there has been far too little emphasis upon the predictions of the Destruction of Jerusalem in 70 AD. Preterists have stressed the utter significance of this event, which closed the era of the Old Covenant and brought to its final end God's dealings with the Jewish nation as such. The UPs have enlightened many who have wondered about some of the passages that pertain to this event (e.g., Matthew 24; Luke 21) and who, as a result, have become enamored with and susceptible to the UP viewpoint. While it is good, in and of itself, to examine the unfounded claims of Futurism, this can be carried too far—even to the point of denying fundamental Christian doctrines. Let me identify some of these.

The UPs deny that there will be a future Second Coming of the Lord Jesus Christ. This, they hold, is an event that has already transpired. The words "Second Coming" may or may not be used by a particular UP, but if he uses it, he always refers to the judgment coming of Christ in 70 AD in which the old order of things was replaced with a new one—the New Testament age. In their view, there is no coming of Christ yet to occur. Samuel Frost writes:

> On the face of it, it would seem ludicrous that anyone would try to defend from the Scriptures and the history of the church that Christ Jesus' Second Coming, the great judgment, and the resurrection of the dead occurred in AD 70.[2]

---

2 Samuel Frost, *Misplaced Hope*. Bimillennial Press: Colorado Springs (2002), p. 13.

Yet that is precisely what he attempts to do throughout the rest of the book and in his newsletter, *The Millennial Post.* The question is not whether the claim that the Second Coming (as well as the other key doctrines mentioned by Frost) occurred in 70 AD is "ludicrous"; rather, the question is whether or not it is scriptural and whether or not such views are orthodox. To refer to UP teaching as possibly viewed as ludicrous in the eyes of many reduces the importance of the issues at stake to mere whimsy. But the matter must not be taken lightly; it is of crucial importance.

Frost goes on to write, "If the Second Coming really did occur in AD 70, does this damage the integrity of the church, her history, and her claim to know the truth?"[3] The OP answer? Absolutely. The vast majority of biblical exegetes have clearly taught the doctrines that UPs reject. If UPs are correct, it would mean that the Bible-believing church would have been deluded or deceived for most of its history, and Christians would have truly entertained a "misplaced hope."

To play down the radical nature of the deviation of UP doctrine from that of the historic church is not only unfortunate, but seems calculated to place those who teach it in the ranks of OPs when, in fact, what they believe is heterodox.[4] To reach back to the apostolic fathers and find "traces" (Frost's term) of his doctrine among them does not lessen the problem. It only minimizes it and confuses the unwary. J. Stuart Russell,[5] upon whose work (*The Parousia)* most of the UPs depend, makes similar claims: "… we

3 *Ibid.*, p. 14.

4 The word means "different from that which is orthodox" (or "straight thinking").

5 J. Stuart Russell (1816–1893) was pastor of the Congregational church at Baswater, England.

conclude that the Parousia,[6] the resurrection, the judgment, and the last day, all belong to the period of the destruction of Jerusalem."[7] Ed Stevens concurs: "Our NT teaches that the 'Parousia,' the resurrection and the judgment were all interconnected events that would occur in the lifetime of those listening to Jesus."[8]

While it is a serious error to explain away the Second Coming as identical with the Judgment Coming of Jesus Christ that *did* occur in 70 AD,[9] the UP is not content to affirm only that error. He is concerned as well to reinterpret the resurrection of the dead by a "spiritual" understanding that eliminates its bodily aspects. On this interpretation, as we have seen in the quotations from Frost and Russell (which are typical of all those in the movement), the UP denies a future resurrection of any buried bodies whatsoever. The hope of the Christian for the transformation of his old body into a new body, which will be conformed to the glorified body of the Lord, is thereby dissolved. The spiritualizing view of the resurrection to which the UP assents trumps the literal one—even though the transformation of the dead body is taught in obviously literal passages such as Philippians 3:21; John 5:28–29; Matthew 27:52. It is *bodies* that are in the graves, that sleep, and that are raised in the resurrection.

---

6 The word *Parousia* is the Greek word used for the advent of Christ. It means "coming, presence or arrival." It was used of a great king upon his arrival in a land.

7 The interrelationship of those doctrines necessitates speaking of all three when dealing primarily with one of them.

8 Ed Stevens, *The International Preterist Association*. Bradford: 1999, pp. 2, 3.

9 Scripture shows that God has frequently "come" in judgment in an invisible coming. See my book *The Time is at Hand* for a fuller explanation of the phrase "Judgment Coming."

As if that were not enough, we see further in the quotations from Frost and Russell that there is (by the UP view) no final judgment following the bodily resurrection of all men from their graves. No, instead, once again, all judgment is relegated to 70 AD.

Let me quote one final comment from John Bray:

> The whole gamut of redemptive prophecy was being fulfilled in those closing days of the Jewish age … Both the first and second appearances of Christ occurred in the closing age of the Jewish age.[10]

These claims must be countered and shown to be false. That they contradict all of the major creeds of the churches is evident. That realization itself should give UPs pause about making such assertions. But they brashly brush creeds aside without trepidation.[11] Yet, it is not enough to wave the creeds before UPs. They speak respectfully about them for the most part, but have no compunction about teaching counter to them when they see fit—even about the most basic doctrines of the church. Because of these facts, as well as others, the UPs must be stopped in their tracks by the

10 John Bray, *Jesus is Coming*. Lakeland: John Bray Ministries (1997), p. 23.

11 Having denied several articles of the creed in asserting their preterist views, there is nothing to hold them back from denying others. John L. Bray, for instance, teaches the annihilation of the wicked and, as a part of that belief, rejects the doctrine of eternal punishment in hell. See *Biblical Perspectives*, Lakeland: June 1, 2002, a publication of which he is the editor. Breach the dyke and the ocean will soon come in.

proper exegesis of Scripture.[12] Nothing else will do. It is to that concern we now turn.

12 Because UP are right in many of their interpretations, and because in these they have good exegesis on their side, they have become cocky about the interpretation of other passages in which they show shoddy and forced exegesis to support untenable teachings.

2

Preterist Exegesis

UP exegesis is highly problematic. Indeed, it is self-contradictory. On the one hand, there is solid—even outstanding—exegesis, while on the other, one finds fanciful and shoddy work. Why is this? How can the same exegetes differ so widely from one passage to another? It is plainly not a matter of competence. Their exegetical abilities are often right on the mark. Some have searched out and found rich insights where others have missed them. Why then the difference? The answer is that where the UPs follow the tried and true path of OP scholarship, they excel. Indeed, some of their exegetical studies, if not brilliant, are masterful. So long as they deal with passages about which all Preterists agree, they rarely go astray. But as soon as they begin to advance their unorthodox views, they make a hash of the Scriptures. In order to maintain their views of the resurrection, the return of Christ, and the judgment, they are forced to arrive at unnatural and uncharacteristic interpretations. They are like someone who has mixed pieces of two different puzzles, trying to make all of the pieces fit. But in order to do so, they find it necessary to cut, shape, and bend some of those pieces.

Let's consider a couple of examples. Russell, the most adroit and satisfying writer among them, does much fine and enlightening work. A good example is how he ties the predictions of John the Baptist with the New Testament passages in which his ministry is described. He rightly characterizes it as having two thrusts, one positive and the other negative. The passage from Isaiah describes his work of announcing the coming of the Savior and His kingdom—a matter of great blessing and joy to all who believe. On the other hand, as set forth in Malachi and actually carried out by John, he also brought a message of judgment upon all who would reject the Lord. Yet when Russell comes to the great commission, because of his desire to fit all of the pieces, he must interpret the word "nations" as "tribes" in Palestine![1] There is no warrant for doing this other than to save his view from being shattered by a passage that really doesn't fit into it.

The UP is up against a difficult task which he often finds he may overcome only by making it happen. What is that task that he has assigned to himself? It is to refer everything—*every* thing—to the period from 33–70 AD. Every prophecy of the Old and the New Testaments must be interpreted to fit this scheme. He dare not allow for even one prophecy to refer to a time subsequent to the destruction of Jerusalem. To do that would utterly destroy his view. Consequently, when a passage truly does find its fulfillment within those prescribed time limits, he is able to freely exegete without any sort of pressure upon him to make the passage fit. That is because it does. He has a piece of the puzzle from the right box. But when he must interpret a passage that actually does not fit his view, somehow or other—like the puzzle player—he must make it do so. This

1 Russell, *op. cit.* "The phrase 'all the nations' is really equivalent to 'all the tribes of the land,' " p. 120.

pressure, as opposed to the freedom to interpret naturally, causes him to distort Scripture.

Consider a second example of this tendency. In many ways, Frost's analysis of the church fathers' beliefs is helpful. On the whole, he correctly sets forth their eschatological viewpoints. At times he may read too much into a portion of their works, but that is rare. Yet, after this useful scholarly work which he has done, at the end he sides with Origen (who was noted for his extravagant allegorizing) in his fanciful interpretation of 1 Corinthians 15:35, 38. These verses respectively read as follows: "But somebody will ask, 'How are the dead raised?' and 'With what sort of body do they come?'" "But God gives it the body that He wants to …" After saying that Origen's interpretation of the passage was "correct," he comments, "Paul mentions two bodies here, one sown, and another given, Adam's body and Christ's body. The 'body' then, that all Christians are raised in, is Christ's."[2]

Of course, in I Corinthians, Paul is speaking of physical, bodily death and resurrection. He is not speaking of the church, the body of Christ. That Frost finds his interpretation questionable and out of line with Paul's thought may be indicated by his including the word body in quotation marks. If he does not feel uncomfortable in agreeing with Origen about this matter, he ought to. To deny the bodily resurrection from the grave, it seems that he found it necessary to grasp at this fanciful interpretation as an expedient.

These are but two examples (picked at random) of the sort of wrong turn that a good exegete takes when he must support a view from a passage that does not comport with

2 *Op. cit.,* p. 138.

it. It is unworthy of him if he knows what he is doing. It is, perhaps, even more sad if he does not. At any rate, the incongruity of finding excellent exegesis alongside highly unacceptable exegesis from the same writer in the same book is clear evidence that passages of Scripture must be bent, cut, and twisted in order to reject major or reinterpret biblical doctrines. Any orthodox Christian who knows his Bible, upon reading UP writings, will certainly recognize the phenomenon to which I am referring.

3

The Second Coming of Christ

Doubtless you have recognized my concern about three main subjects upon which UPs and OPs disagree. These are the Second Coming of Jesus Christ, the bodily resurrection, and the judgment (including, of course, the intermediate and eternal states). There are other differences about which there might be discussion, but if there is a resolution of these matters, the others would follow in course. Therefore, I plan to take up each of these issues in succession.

It is the contention of the UPs that there is no second coming of Christ—at least as the church has taught it. Rather, all passages which are customarily referred to as the second coming ought to be referred to as the judgment coming of Jesus Christ upon Israel in 70 AD. Let it be said right now—the church has been remiss in its consideration of that important event. The significance of the destruction of Jerusalem to an understanding of God's plan in history must not be underplayed. Here was a great focal point in time: the point at which the people of God, who formerly had been the theocracy of Israel, now took on a new and different form. The old Sinaitic covenant was replaced by the New Covenant made with the new Israel, the church. This new people of God included Gentiles,[1] as well as a remnant of believing Jews. With the destruction of Jerusalem and the bringing down of the temple, the old order of things passed forever. Animal sacrifice was ended now that the once-for-all sacrifice of Jesus Christ on Calvary had been completed. His cry, "It is finished," was no cry of relief. Rather, it was a declaration that all He had come to do had been completed (as the word translated "finished" in the KJV means).

This failure of the church to adequately address the event that took place in 70 AD has left the door wide open to the UP. And he has stepped through it. Why has the church neglected this important happening? God providentially raised up Josephus, who, having been in both the Jewish and the Roman camps, recorded in depth the course of the war, the details of the destruction, and the final defeat of Israel. More concern seems to have been given to the matter by Josephus than by the church, which, after the interim from 33–70 AD, finally came fully into its own. The church, in a real sense, began anew as it was completely freed from its Jewish shackles by the judgment upon the temple and the nation of Israel.

This age-shaking event was prophesied in the Old Testament as well as in the New. But the Jews failed to heed the warnings in Deuteronomy and thus became subject to the curses pronounced there (cf. Deuteronomy 28). Their land was taken away from them, and their nation was replaced by a people who had not been a nation (Matthew 21:43; 1 Peter 2:9, 10). Jesus spoke of the destruction in His Olivet discourse (Luke 21; Matthew 24), and there are references to the event scattered throughout the New Testament books.

1 The word translated "Gentiles" is, actually, "Nations." It referred to non-Jews.

Yet, in spite of its prominence and importance in Scripture, the destruction of Jerusalem has not been emphasized by the church as it should have been. As a result, a number of the passages that predict the end of the old era and the coming of a new one, instead, have been wrongly referred to as the Second Coming. Passages that speak of the "end of the age" or the "latter days" have been understood as having to do with the latter or last days of our times rather than the last days of the Old Testament era. Add to these problems a dash of Dispensational eschatology, and you have a confusing prophetic stew.

The UPs, as well as the OPs, have rightly pointed to the significance of the change of world order that occurred in 70 AD. They have properly exegeted many verses that have been wrongly applied to the Second Coming, correctly assigning them to the destruction coming of Christ that occurred in 70 AD. As a result, more and more people in recent times have become interested in the careful interpretation of the Scriptures emanating from OP quarters. Because of the work done by Preterists in salvaging the true meaning of many verses that were wrongly applied to the future, however, these interested people have become prey for other UP teachings. Recognizing the truth of the Preterist interpretation of these passages, unfortunately, has led some to the uncritical acceptance of UP doctrine that is false. Just because the UPs, like all Preterists, have rightly understood some (even many) passages does not mean that they have correctly understood all of them. If the expression "throwing out the baby with the bath water" ever applied to any situation, it certainly applies to the UP assertion that all prophecies have been fulfilled. This is the consistent UP theme. John L. Bray writes,

> Both the first and the second appearance of Christ occurred in the closing days of the Jewish age … the whole New Testament teaches that Jesus Christ was to return in the first century.[2]

Max King says,

> There is not the slightest indication that any of the Old Testament promises were taken up in the New Testament and continued unfulfilled beyond the end of the Jewish age, or that the New Testament contains a new set of promises to be fulfilled beyond the Christian age.[3]

In this statement, the Second Coming, the judgment, and the bodily resurrection are in one sweep of the broom whisked away from consideration. King further declares, "NOTHING was postponed. NOTHING was carried into the Christian age unfulfilled."[4]

In a brochure published by the International Preterist Association entitled, "What Is The Preterist View?" Edward Stevens, president of the association, is quoted as saying, "Scripture foretells a Second Coming (Hebrews 9:28)—not a third!" By those words, he means that the destruction in 70 AD *was* the second coming of Christ, and that there is now no future coming that Christians should look forward to.

John Noe, in a book designed to show how the Preterist view answers various kinds of critics, wrote, "When a

---

2 John L. Bray, *Jesus is Coming Soon*! Jn.L.Bray Ministry, Pubs., Lakeland: n.d., pp. 23, 40.
3 Max R. King, *Old Testament Israel and New Testament Salvation*. Eschatology Pubs, Warren: n.d., p.3.
4 *Ibid.*, p. 71 [capitals his].

Christian first hears a statement that ... Jesus has returned (past tense), he or she, most likely, will react in a knee-jerk fashion."[5] Noe is right about that! His concern to answer the critics on the whole is admirable and certainly warrants careful consideration. The problem is not to answer the critics who say that the Bible (and Jesus) was wrong in predicting a coming in the lifetime of the apostles by showing He came in judgment coming, but in doing so, like other UPs, Noe makes *all* prophecies of *every* coming the basis for his argument. We shall show that it is unnecessary (as well as unscriptural) to do this. But for now, note the import of his words, "Jesus has returned." He doesn't mean that the coming in the judgment coming of 70 AD will be followed someday by a coming of Jesus to bring an end to the present order of things, but that the coming in 70 AD *was the only coming* that was predicted, and that it fulfilled all possible expectations that are usually associated with the Second Coming. We have no difficulty using his argument so far as it follows the Scriptures, but we depart from it when he says that every passage having to do with a coming of Jesus was fulfilled in the destruction of Jerusalem. Why OPs and UPs disagree and why the distinction between the two Preterist camps must be made and maintained will be considered in the chapters that follow.

5 John Noe, *Dead in Their Tracks*. International Preterist Assn., Bradford (2001), p. 25.

4

Why Another Coming?

If the Unorthodox Preterists are correct, we must rewrite the creeds.[1] But no one should even think of doing that except for the strongest reasons imaginable. Their attempt to do so ought to offer cause for pause. We all know about churches that have departed from the historic Reformation faith because they refused to heed the truth of God summarized in the creeds. Most of the time, it is wise to heed the creeds. When, on a rare occasion, one believes that he is compelled to do so, the question constantly in his mind must be, "Am I really sure?" And the UP must ask himself, "Is there sufficient scriptural reason to warrant a rejection of every creed that speaks of the return of Jesus Christ in a final judgment after his body has been raised from the grave at the end of *our* age?" It is my opinion that it is not possible, biblically speaking, to eliminate or alter the creedal views of the Reformation churches regarding the Second Coming.

The UPs have a lot of incontrovertible facts on their side regarding the proper interpretation of passages that have been wrongly understood as having to do with the Second Coming (eg, the prophecy in Matthew 24). That must be granted. I do not intend to rehearse them in this place.

1 To tag the "Full Preterists" with the label "Unorthodox" is to declare that they do not abide by the orthodoxy set forth in the creeds.

Rather, the arguments supporting their views are found in nearly every one of their books, where they are rehashed over and over again. When Jesus said that He would come in His generation and that some of His disciples would be alive at that coming, there is no exegetically acceptable way to interpret His words but to declare that He meant just that (despite the many attempts to show otherwise). Jesus was saying that He would come to destroy Jerusalem, not at some distant time, thousands of years into the future, but shortly, before the end of the Old Testament era, which closed in 70 AD. All of that may be acknowledged without giving up the orthodox doctrines of the coming of Christ at the time of the resurrection and the final judgment of men. How can this be? Now, let us consider His coming, or *Parousia*.

To begin with, think for a moment about Jesus' ascension into heaven. The passage in Acts 1:9–11 describes this remarkable scene (also referred to in Acts 1:22; 2:33–34). Here is what Luke wrote:

> *When He had said this, He was taken up as they watched; a cloud took Him up from their sight. As they were gazing at the sky while He went, two men in white clothes stood by them and said, "Men of Galilee, why do you stand looking at the sky? This Jesus who has been taken up from you will come back in the same way that you saw Him go into the sky."*

Now, in light of this passage, all of the objections that are leveled at Jesus coming in the air to receive His own should be laid aside. Rather, because of these verses just quoted from the book of Acts, one should acknowledge, if no more, that the idea is entirely plausible. After all, as He predicted in John 6:62, Christ visibly left the earth by being caught up in a cloud. That this was literally a bodily ascension is plain from the fact that afterward the disciples stood gazing at the sky. However remarkable it may seem, there is nothing implausible about glorified human bodies being lifted up into the air. Jesus' body was! So, the scorn that is sometimes cast upon those who teach the "rapture"[2] of believers, as if this were ludicrous, ought to be abandoned.[3] While rejecting the two-part future coming of pretribulation Premillennialists—first for the saints and then later for the rest of the dead—there is no reason to abandon the idea of Jesus coming back *from the sky.* As we later consider 1 Thessalonians 4:13ff., we shall find further evidence which must cause us to conclude that this is precisely what will happen.

Looking further into the Acts account, we encounter the important words of the angels:[4] "This Jesus, Who has been taken up from you, will come back in the same way that you saw Him go into the sky."[5] That Jesus predicted He would come in judgment in 70 AD cannot be seriously doubted. All Preterists believe and teach that. But that this judgment coming precludes a different sort of coming of Jesus in the future is not refuted by that fact.[6] Indeed, Jesus

2 The word in Acts describing the mode of the ascension simply means snatching or catching up.

3 Some of the sarcasm about airplanes hitting Christians "floating" in clouds over the earth, etc., found in Bray's book, *The Rapture of Christians* is unworthy of him. Elsewhere, his writing, whether correct or not, is calm, reasoned and reasonable.

4 As a side comment, here, as elsewhere, angels always assume the form of men.

5 In Acts 2:33, 34 the ascension "into the heavens" is said to eventuate in Christ's exaltation to the Father's "right hand."

6 There are numerous judgment comings of God mentioned in the Old Testament. Therefore, there is no reason to object to more than one in the New Testament.

did come back to destroy Jerusalem and the temple within the city. But His coming in judgment was nothing like what is described here by the angels. His coming in judgment in 70 AD was invisible; only its effects were seen. That means that in that event, He did not come "in like manner," or "in the same way," as the angels predicted He would. Were the angels wrong? Of course not! They were speaking of another future event that is distinct from the coming in 70 AD. The ascension, in which Jesus departed from the apostles by rising into the air and disappearing into a cloud, was a visible event. To accept this account is to accept the fact that it could happen again—this time to believers.

Significantly, there is no mention of judgment in what Luke wrote in Acts 1. Whereas the coming to destroy Jerusalem is described as a judgment poured out upon unrepentant and wicked Jews, the Second Coming announced by the angels carried none of these overtones. This fact means that judgment was not the prime factor as it was in 70 AD. Indeed, if anything, it would seem that by their words, they comforted the startled and fearful disciples. At any rate, there is not a single angelic word of judgment associated with Jesus' return, which is described as coming "in the same way."[7]

In his Gospel, Luke throws further light on the ascension by revealing that the angels associated blessing with the re-

---

7 The word *tropos* translated, "in the same way," means *in the same fashion or manner.* Literally, the Greek reads, "in what manner (or way)." As Souter puts it in his Lexicon, "in the way in which." *Tropos* is used in Hebrews 13:5 where it carries the idea of a manner of living. The manner in which Jesus will return must be in a manner that is similar to that in which He left the disciples. Alexander notes that "The Greek phrase never indicates mere certainty or vague resemblance; but wherever it occurs in the New Testament denotes identity of mode or manner." J.A. Alexander, *The Acts of the Apos-*

turn of Jesus from heaven. Speaking of Jesus, he wrote: "He lifted up His hands and blessed them. As He was blessing them, He withdrew from them [and was carried up into heaven]" (Luke 24:50-51). While the bracketed words are omitted from some manuscripts, the evidence for their inclusion is strong.

But apart from the textual matter, it is plain that on this occasion, Jesus left the disciples while *blessing* them. The return these two passages speak about would not be primarily[8] a return in judgment but a return of blessing. In every way, then, the "manner" of coming back to judge Jerusalem in 70 AD and Christ's future return to bless His people are plainly differentiated. Nothing about the Judgment Coming and the Second Coming described[9] by Luke is identical. They refer to two distinct events in which Jesus is said to return—each for different purposes and, consequently, in different ways. In various passages, we are told that Jesus will come again, but the unmistakable fact is that not all of Christ's comings are described as happening "in the same way." We must now consider in greater depth what the Bible reveals about this coming for His own in blessing.

tles. The Banner of Truth Trust: Edinburgh (1991), p.16.

8 Judgment of the wicked will occur at the Second Coming; here only blessing for His own is mentioned.

9 Luke's description of the judgment in Jerusalem is found in chapter 21 of his gospel.

5

A Fuller Look at Jesus' Second Coming

In 1 Thessalonians 4:13 and following, Paul provides a fuller look at the final coming of Jesus Christ. It is clearly identical with that which is predicted in Acts 1. As we saw, Jesus will come "in the same way" that He left His disciples. Here, in I Thessalonians, we have a description of how He will do so. It is a bodily, visible coming that is described by the apostle Paul. It involves Jesus descending from the sky into which He had previously ascended. And it is a blessed event for His own. Here are Paul's words:

> *Now, we don't want you to be ignorant, brothers, about those who sleep, lest you grieve as others who haven't any hope. If we believe that Jesus died and rose again, in the same way, through Jesus, God also will bring with Him those who sleep. This we say to you by the Lord's Word, that we who remain alive until the coming of the Lord will not get ahead of those who are asleep. The Lord Himself will descend from the sky with an assembling shout, with the voice of the archangel, and with the trumpet of God, and the dead in Christ will rise first, then we who remain alive shall be caught up together with them in the clouds as an escort to welcome the Lord as he comes into the air, and so shall we always be with the Lord (1 Thessalonians 4:13–17).*

Of significance are the following facts:

1. The passage is included in a didactic (not an apocalyptic or symbolic) section of Scripture. The attempts of some UPs to "spiritualize" away the facts presented by Paul are highly suggestive of their need to circumvent the obvious intention of his words. Paul is comforting Christians about the future of their loved ones who have died. He is not giving them some cryptic explanation of the Lord's coming. Instead, he is attempting to assuage their grief by replacing "ignorance" with plain facts. There is something almost cruel to suggest otherwise. These Christians needed factual data to be able to grieve as Christians should, in contrast to unbelievers who have no hope. The passage, then, is intended to give hope.

2. In the fourteenth verse we read the interesting words, "in the same way." The original Greek literally says, "so also." In other words, there is a correspondence between the death and resurrection of Christ and the death and resurrection of the believer. The correspondence between the two is reminiscent of the correspondence noted by the angels in Acts 1. As Jesus died and rose from the dead in His bodily form to glory and honor, "so also" shall the dead in Christ rise and be glorified. As He parted into the sky in a physical, visible, tangible body, "so also" He will return from the sky in a visible, physical way.

3. But the descent of the Lord Jesus as He comes back to earth will not merely be a coming into the air. At that time He will assemble His own by calling them forth from the grave (or changing them, if still alive) so as to meet Him in the air. Why do the believers go out *to meet* Christ as He returns to earth? Certainly not to hang around in the air for seven years before He actually comes to the earth. No. The word "meet" is a specialized term used in only two other places in the New Testament (mentioned below). It does not refer to the sort of meeting that takes place when two people happen to meet while walking down the street. Nor does it refer to a called meeting—say, of a church board of elders. It is a specialized term meaning "to meet *in order to escort back*."

In Acts 28:15 we read that "the brothers from there, when they heard about us, came as far as the Appian Forum and the Three Taverns to welcome and escort us back." In Matthew 25:1 (a passage that has to do with Christ the Bridegroom's coming) we read, "At that time the empire from the heavens will be likened to ten virgins who took their lamps and went out to meet and escort the bridegroom." And when the bridegroom came at midnight, we learn that this is precisely what they did (vv. 6–10). The word *apantesis* was used, says Souter, as "a phrase seemingly almost technical for the reception of a newly arrived official." Even today the custom persists. When a foreign dignitary arrives in Washington, a greeting party goes out to the airfield to welcome him and escort him from the plane to the White House. The reason why believers are snatched up to meet the Lord in the air, then, is to honor Him as *the* Dignitary of dignitaries and escort Him back at His return to earth.

4. The use of the word "we" in the passage has been interpreted by UPs to indicate that Paul was speaking about his own day. But Paul could not have included himself in the group that would "remain alive" until the Lord's return because he was to die (2 Timothy 4:6: "the time for my departure has arrived").[1] Doubtless, instead, Paul identified

1 True, the letter to Timothy was written after that to the Thessalonians. But, since I Thessalonians was inspired revelation, Paul

himself with all believers just the way *we* do when we say, "We do" (as I just did!).

Now let us take a closer look at the passage before us. In it, we have a clear statement that the Lord would come again. In this statement, Paul is speaking to Christians living far from Palestine who had lost (or who would lose) their loved ones. Surely, in this context he had no reason whatsoever to refer to the destruction of Jerusalem. But he had every reason to speak about a time when dead Christians would rise, together with those who remain until Christ's return. He wrote to comfort them (v. 18). To suggest otherwise is to declare that Paul wrote about a matter that was wholly irrelevant to his readers. Referring the 1 Thessalonians 4 event to the judgment coming in 70 AD is to introduce elements foreign to it. Doing so misses the point of the passage.

According to Bray, the resurrection began when Christ returned "in the First Century."[2] And according to him, it is not over: "It is a continuing process."[3] What is such a resurrection, anyway? "That resurrection which took place at the coming of Jesus years ago continues on today as each Christian sheds his earthly body to receive a new body from Heaven."[4] Bray thinks that we have been "brainwashed into believing that being 'caught up' (raptured) means something for the living human beings. Being caught up … is the same as being resurrected."[5] It is not the "levitation of the physical body into the air, but rather, it is the Christian

could not have been mistaken, finding it necessary to correct his earlier prediction later on.

2 *The Rapture of Christians*, *op. cit.*, p. 9.
3 *Ibid.*, p. 11.
4 *Ibid.*, p. 12.
5 *Ibid.*, p. 13.

himself being caught up into the heavenly[6] atmosphere. He leaves his old body and takes on his new body."[7]

How strange this teaching is! The resurrection is not a corporate event, as Paul clearly described it, but rather, an individual one for each believer throughout history. Surely, the description as given by Bray and others doesn't do justice to the words of Paul. It looks like a dodge—a way of escaping from the true teaching of 1 Thessalonians 4 in order to uphold the UP position. And it contradicts Paul as well. Paul says that the living believer who is caught up will not "go ahead" of those who sleep (v. 15). And he says that the living Christian will be caught up "together" with those who have died. But if that's so, there is no continuing resurrection even up to our time and beyond; in 1 Thessalonians 4 *all* are "caught up" *together*.

If the rapture *is* the resurrection, and the resurrection is not a physical one but a coming into a new body, then Paul's description of the facts is misleading, if not incorrect. In contrast to the UP theory, Paul *does* picture the assembling of believers who, together as a welcoming body, go out to meet their Lord in the air and escort Him back to the earth. That word *apantesis* ("to meet in order to escort back") must be reckoned with. The resurrection for Paul is not an unending series of individual experiences that still continues; it is a one-time event in which all meet as a grand escort for Jesus. Jesus does not come to be escorted back to earth again and again at the death of each Christian! The fact is that the words of Paul are totally incongruous with Bray's theory.

---

6 N.B., Bray says "heavenly," not earthly, atmosphere.

7 *Ibid.*, p.13. Note the wording here, it is crucial. The "old body" is not transformed. Rather, according to Bray, what takes place is the substitution of a new body for the old one. By "the Christian himself" he means the human spirit, apart from the body.

More could be said about the Second Coming, but the proper understanding of the two events (the ascension and the Second Coming to raise the dead and change the living) is sufficient to set this matter straight. There is no satisfactory way to substitute the UP theory for the biblical truth. It must be rejected out of hand.

6

More About His Coming

In 1 Thessalonians 4:14 we read,

> *If we believe that Jesus died and rose again, in the same way, through Jesus, God also will bring with Him those who sleep.*

We have already studied those words to an extent, but now we shall focus on the fact that Paul taught the Thessalonian Christians that God, through Jesus, would "bring with Him"[1] those Christians who had died. The means, or agent, by whom the souls of these Christians should come to the great meeting in the air is Christ coming again. It is "through [by means of] Him" that God brings them on that occasion as they come "together with Him."[2] That is to say, this event is accomplished through Christ's power or agency as He "descends" together with the spirits of these Christians who have died. We know that it is their spirits that will accompany Jesus since their *bodies* have been "sleeping" in their graves. The way in which they will escort Him back to earth at His coming, therefore, necessitates a bodily resurrection involving the possession of transformed bodies.

1 Literally, "lead together with Him."
2 The preposition used is *sun* which means "together with" or "in the company of."

But their disembodied spirits must have previously been in heaven in order to come "together with Him."[3] Soul sleep is ruled out by this fact. Paul's concern in the passage is to show that dead Christians will not be deprived of anything that those who will be living at the time of Jesus' return will enjoy. He is not interested in all the details of the Second Coming. Nevertheless, many of his assumptions concerning it appear as the basis for his words.

As I mentioned, the "we" in verses 15 and 17 ("we who remain") has been used by some UPs to infer from this use of the first person that the coming *had* to be in Paul's lifetime. Commenting on the "we" passages, John Noe, for instance, writes, "Paul wasn't writing to some far-distant generation of people.... Paul speaks personally and contemporarily, not editorially."[4] But, as many commentators have observed, Paul is simply viewing the coming as one who, at the time of writing, is living (since he still was) rather than identifying with the second class of believers ("the dead in Christ," v. 16). "We" means people who, *like us now,* are alive when Jesus comes again. To put it in Noe's terms, speaking "editorially" is precisely what Paul was doing. It would have been unnecessary to say something like, "You who are living" as over against "we who will at that coming be dead."[5] The fact is that, in using the word "we," he was not talking about himself (or even primarily about those to whom he was writing) but about those who had died—what would happen to them, as over against those who will

3 Notice how the event is described as the spirits of believers accompanying Jesus at His coming. How can such a description be equated with the destruction of Jerusalem?
4 The reader must not miss Paul's similar use of the first person in 1 Corinthians 15:51, 52.
5 John Noe, *op. cit.*, p. 19.

remain alive until His coming. That was the concern of the Thessalonian believers. They may well have wrongly believed that Christ would come in their lifetime—this may have been the reason for their question about the fate of dead Christians.[6] That does not say that Paul believed it.

Note also how the ascension (discussed in a previous chapter) corresponds so fully with the Second Coming depicted by Paul. Both events are described as personal, visible, and bodily. Both are accompanied by clouds. In the one, Jesus ascends into the sky; in the second, He descends into the air.[7] There is a distinct similarity to the two events as we saw in Acts 1. To deny this is to exhibit a bias that screens out the obvious meaning of words.

Once again, the question might be asked, "Why should Christians be 'snatched up' into the air"? (v. 17). Why do they "rise"? (v. 16). The answer is to meet and escort the Lord Jesus back to earth in accordance with His promise. This is presumably the time when they come back with Him to "judge men and angels" (1 Corinthians 6:2–3). At any rate, the Lord Jesus is coming back with His saints, and it is that time when the final judgment of all men will occur. This doctrine is also distorted by the UPs. So, we must begin to consider it in the next chapter.

---

6 In his second letter, Paul must caution his readers not to think Christ had already come (2 Thessalonians 2:1–3).

7 Noe attempts to make a point of the fact that in Acts the word for "heaven" or "sky" is used, while in I Thessalonians Paul uses the word "air" (pp. 23ff.). Actually, the word *ouranos*, used in Acts, *includes* the air. Often it is in the plural, clearly indicating the fact that it comprised more than one referent (the atmosphere, the sky of stars and planets and the dwelling place of God). Here, one of those three is mentioned—the air (or atmosphere). That neither of the other two could have been in the disciples' mind is clear from the fact that they watched Jesus ascend until a cloud took Him up out of sight. The clouds, and that which is beneath them, is the air!

7

No Resurrection of the Body?

That, believe it or not, is what UPs teach! Your dead body will not be raised physically from a grave. Obviously, this well-established and cardinal doctrine of the faith—the resurrection of the body—must be rejected if they are to hold to their view that all has been accomplished already—even the resurrection of the dead. Max King writes, "in regard to *bodily* resurrection, we believe there is a reasonable and scriptural alternative view of the traditional *physical* or *biological* resurrection view(s)."[1] What is it? King also writes,

> The paramount issue here is not what God can or cannot do, but what is the meaning and function of the resurrection that was "preached through Jesus." Does it relate to the recovery of decomposed physical bodies at the end of time, planet earth, or human existence, or was it tied to the climax of redemptive history[2] in terms of man's redemption and restoration to God? Is it connected to a change in man's bodily form and substance, or does it pertain to a change in

1 Max King, *The Cross and the Parousia of Christ.* Writing and Research Ministry: Warren (1987), p. 382.

2 King defends his biblical-theological view on the basis of redemptive history.

> man's mode of existence in this life that gives man life and immortality now through putting on Christ? It is clear that the latter view has the overwhelming support of Scripture.[3]

John Noe adds, "during the biblical 'last days' (Hebrews 1:2), which occurred in the middle of the 1st Century, the dead were raised."[4] Obviously, that event could not have been a physical resurrection. According to him, Old Testament believers were "raised out of Hades, the holding place of the dead."[5] But what of believers who were alive at the coming in 70 AD? Noe has an answer: "it's straight to heaven and into God's Presence in the Holy of Holies for the Christian, directly and immediately, upon physical death."[6] Here are a series of statements by Noe explaining what he means:

> The thought of a physically resurrected old body is not to be found here or anywhere in Scripture.... I don't know about you, but like Paul (Ph. 3:10–16; Rm. 8:23), I'm looking forward to getting my new resurrection body immediately after I die ... the ingredients of a believer's new spiritual body are contained inside the old natural body. At our new birth, our spirit is indwelt by God. It begins

3 *Ibid.*, p. 666.
4 John Noe, *Shattering the Left Behind Delusion.* IPA, Pub.: Bradford, n.d. p.59.
5 *Ibid.*, p. 76. But, in a recent change of views, Stevens has come to believe that there was a bodily resurrection and rapture at the destruction of Jerusalem. He thinks that is why we have no written, contemporary evidence of the event. All of those who were raised and could have written about it were gone! But would no Christians living immediately afterwards have commented? It is a strange view that hardly needs refutation. Bray disagrees with Stevens (though not mentioning him by name), and in his July 8, 2002 newsletter, *Biblical Perspectives*, Lakeland, p. 3, refutes the idea.
6 *Ibid.*, p. 97.

> to grow and rise up within. Then one day it will break out into the fabric of our new spiritual body. That's a continuity. But the new body is different from the seed [physical] body. That's a discontinuity.[7]

So the resurrection "body" is no more than the spiritual life of the believer now grown up and (perhaps) perfected at death. The resurrection is not one great event, but a never-ending series of mini-events that occur whenever believers die.[8] The 70 AD event merely made this possible and certain. That is the view as Noe sees it. Now, what shall we say about all of this?

First, such teachings are unorthodox and justify the title "*Unorthodox* Preterists" (UPs), which I have given to the full Preterists. Be that as it may, what is of significance is what the Bible has to say; that, in the final analysis, is the only question that matters. Note the supposed ongoing nature of the resurrection at the death of each believer. Those individual mini-events hardly accord with the great event described in 1 Thessalonians 4:13ff. where the trumpet sounds, all believers rise into the air, and Jesus Christ is revealed in all His splendor. Noe and others believe this was the gathering

7 *Ibid.*, pp. 128, 133, 134 (bracketed word mine). Does the future body of the lost grow up and rise again within him? Or does Noe think that the wicked are annihilated?

8 As Bray put it, "The resurrection of Christians began when Christ returned in the first century." *The Rapture of Christians*. John Bray Ministry pub.: Lakeland (1998), p. 9. He says further, "the resurrection is not over … It is a continuing process," p. 11. He then goes on for several pages to teach conditional immortality, the view that man is not by nature immortal, but that immortality is granted only to those who trust in Christ. Prior to the "resurrection" he says, "All of Christ's people rose out of sleep, put on their new bodies and became immortal" (p. 17). Moreover, on pp. 27, 34 he clearly teaches soul sleep. Old Testament believers [not just their bodies] remained in sheol (as he understands it, the grave) until given immortality at the resurrection in 70 AD.

of Old Testament saints from Hades when they were taken into heaven. The reasons for this are so slim as not to give them a hearing. But listen to the apostle Paul, who in Romans 8:18–23 wrote:

> *For this reason, I don't count the sufferings of this present time worthy of comparison with the glory that is going to be revealed to us. The creation anxiously awaits, eagerly anticipating the revelation of God's sons. The entire creation was subjected to futility, not because it wanted to be, but because of the One Who subjected it with the hope that the creation itself will be set free from its slavery to corruption and realize the glorious freedom of God's children. We know that the entire creation groans together in labor pains until now. And not only the creation, but we ourselves who have the Spirit as a firstfruit also groan inwardly as we eagerly await our adoption, that is, our bodily redemption.*

In conjunction with this passage, the body was said to be awaiting its redemption together with all creation. On that occasion, those things that had suffered corruption would be "set free" from the slavery that corruption brought about. King and others interpret the passage as believers awaiting the 70 AD coming, not the future advent of Christ. According to UPs, the group in view is Old Testament saints (not all believers), and the creation is unbelievers. That what we groan about is sin, and not the curse upon the physical body, is hard to countenance. And how would the unbelieving world groan and look forward to the redemption of the body of sin? King's answer is that there was an expectancy of the heathen world at the time of Christ that something unique would happen. There was such an expectation, but to equate the two is far-fetched.

Now you can see to what exegetical lengths UPs go to establish their position. There is no indication whatsoever that the body mentioned in Romans 8 is anything other than the physical body in which we all groan because of the effects of sin upon it—sickness, deformities, disease, death. The firstfruit mentioned is the Spirit of God Who seals (identifies) us for the Redemption Day as God's. We belong to Him. How can it be that, according to King, the creation (world of unsaved persons) eagerly awaits the revelation of God's sons? The idea is preposterous. That which occurs at the resurrection is the redemption of the physical body for believers, which demonstrates their adoption as God's children. This is plainly set forth in Ephesians 4:20: "And don't grieve God's Holy Spirit with Whom you were sealed for the redemption day." The Spirit is like an earnest, a mark that we who are His belong to Him, an indication that some day God will redeem us as His own. That is what Paul had in mind. And the "creation" is the world and all in it that has been affected negatively by the curse.

What truly informs our understanding of the 1 Thessalonians 4:13ff. and Romans 8 passages that we have been studying? It is the bodily change that will take place at the coming of the Lord Jesus. Paul wrote,

> *But our citizenship is in the heavens, from which country we await the coming of a Savior, the Lord Jesus Christ, Who will transform our degraded bodies, making them to conform to His glorious body (Philippians 3:20, 21).*[9]

9 Don't miss the fact that the present body will be "transformed" (or "refashioned") at Christ's coming. Paul does not speak of substituting a new body for the old one.

The body's "slavery to corruption" (mentioned in Romans 8) was what he had in mind when he penned that statement. Because of the effects of sin and the curse, the body has become degraded. Man, who ought to be able to subdue the earth, instead, is subdued by it and is finally returned to dust. The body is degraded by all of the ills of this life: disease, injury, deformity, and the like—including death, which is the ultimate degradation. Paul looked forward to a time when his body would conform to Christ's risen body, which, being freed from the slavery of corruption, was glorified and made capable of remarkable acts—but it was still visible and tangible. In the Philippians passage, we are also told, in harmony with Acts 1 and 1 Thessalonians 4, that we await the coming of Jesus Christ *from the heavens.* And, again in perfect harmony with them, that is when our degraded bodies will be changed to conform to Christ's risen body. Words could hardly be clearer. No convoluted system needs to be placed upon them in order to make them fit a theory.

The body of Jesus Christ was raised from the grave, physically. In it, He appeared, spoke, and ate with the disciples for over forty days (Acts 1:3–4; 10:39–41). They were able to recognize it and touch it: "See My hands and My feet that I am Myself. Touch me and see, because a spirit doesn't have flesh and bones as you see I have" (Luke 24:39). If our spiritual bodies are to be like His glorified body, we too shall have bodies that are visible and tangible. The bodily resurrection, like Christ's, will be from the grave (not from within)![10]

---

10 The past resurrection of believers of which we have knowledge was precisely like Christ's resurrection: "The graves were opened up and many of the bodies of those who had fallen asleep were

Well, is that all? Certainly not. Listen to the apostle John:

> *Dear friends, we are God's children now, but it doesn't yet appear what we shall be. We know that when it does appear we shall be like Him, because we shall see Him as He is (1 John 3:2 [italics mine]).*

Those words, once again, conform to the words of Paul in Philippians 3; Romans 8: and 1 Thessalonians 4. The solid, uniform biblical presentation of the facts, such as we have seen here, ought to cause believers to look forward to a coming resurrection of the body in which it is transformed (i.e., glorified so as to become a spiritual body, which means that it is directed wholly by the Spirit). It will be free from all of the ills occasioned by the fall. And it will not be a second body, but the first and only body that a believer will ever have,[11] now refashioned to become like the Lord's body. It will have remarkable new powers. Using these new abilities, like our Lord, we too shall ascend in these newly-made bodies to meet and escort the Lord as He comes. Nothing less than this does justice to the passages considered, which passages, when properly exegeted, prove the UP system to be utterly bankrupt.

---

raised, they were raised out of their graves—and appeared to many" (Matthew 27:52, 53). Clearly what came out of the graves (literally, "tombs") was bodies that had been previously buried.

11 Jesus resurrected body was the same body (now glorified) that was placed in the tomb.

8

The Resurrection

So far, our interest has been the bodily resurrection of Jesus Christ from the dead and His visible, physical return. That He declared to the disciples that He had flesh and bones (Luke 24:39–40) and invited the disciples to touch Him makes it certain that He wanted us to know that He had risen *bodily*. Add to that the fact that Jesus ate and drank with the disciples after His resurrection (Acts 10:40). These recorded facts, in and of themselves, clinch the matter. If anyone cannot see that, he is hopelessly biased against the physical resurrection of the same body as the one that was buried.

But having shown that Jesus' resurrection from the grave was a bodily one, it remains to be established from the Scriptures that we, who are believers in Him, likewise will be raised bodily sometime in the future. I have already mentioned earlier Paul's words in Philippians 3:21 where he declares in clear and unmistakable terms that Jesus Christ will "transform our degraded (or humiliated) bodies" by "conforming them to His glorious body." Note, it is our *present bodies* that will be transformed. Since this is true, they cannot remain moldering in the grave at the resurrection. The Greek terminology in that verse is not only interesting but instructive. And the context is equally so.

Paul is encouraging his readers, unlike those who "think only about earthly things" (v. 19) to recognize that they hold their prime "citizenship in heaven" (v. 20). The implication of this is that they should "await the coming of a Savior, the Lord Jesus Christ" (v. 20). That is to say, He is in the heavens (elsewhere said to be at the right hand of God), in this heavenly country of which we are citizens, and from which He will return to earth to transform our bodies (now degraded by sin) so that they will become like His body of glory (v. 21). That is to say, these bodies will be made fit to dwell in the heavenly city. That is the context. Jesus is now in the heavenly country. He will come from there, and He will give us bodies just like His (bodies that are visible, tangible, physical, as we just saw in the paragraphs above). The likeness of the believer's transformed body to Christ's glorified body upon His return is plainly taught.

The believer's citizenship already "exists," Paul says. The word used is *huparko*, which denotes an already existing situation or condition. It is not that we are granted this citizenship when Jesus returns, but that we have it already by virtue of our salvation. The One Who saved us and granted this gift of citizenship by grace will come again. Believers "await" this event, at which time we shall receive our newly transformed bodies. The word *apodexomai*[1] pictures someone patiently awaiting the coming of another. Now, UPs, as usual, latch on to the first-person usage "we, our." See, they say, Paul includes himself, so this event must be one that he expected in his lifetime. They think it poses an insuperable problem for anyone who awaits a future coming of Christ. I have already dealt with this so-called problem elsewhere.

1 This is the same verb as that which is used in Romans 8:23.

Paul was speaking about and to living Christians of every era and thus included himself. It is an inclusive first person. This is a common biblical usage, and we should not press it to say more than was intended.[2]

Note what will happen: He will "transform our degraded bodies" at the time when our expectations are fulfilled by His coming from the heavenly country. Certainly, that did not take place in 70 AD. The term, *metaschematizo*, means to "refashion, change, transform, change the form of." It is a powerful term which indicates that at the Savior's return, a great alteration in our bodily condition will occur. Something must exist already in order to be transformed! The term has in it the idea of "transforming something ... into something wholly different."[3] Here, the transformation is from a body that is humiliated by sin and the curse into one that is "glorious"—as glorious as is the risen body of Christ. It is the *same body* in both cases. This event is something that happens to all who have trusted Him as their "Savior." Nothing like this happened in 70 AD or since.[4] Obviously, it is yet future. And the time at which it occurs is identified as the time when Jesus comes from the heavenly country. To transform corrupted bodies, Paul intimates, requires divine "power." It is a power by which He can "subject all things to Himself." That would include the changing of degraded living bodies and disintegrated buried ones. Obviously,

---

2 Notice how in this very sentence I used the word "we." I included the reader. Surely when he wrote that "our citizenship is in heaven" he didn't wish to exclude those of other periods than his own. The "our" includes all believers as *over against* unbelievers.

3 Rienecker/Rogers, *Linguistic Key to the Greek New Testament*. Zondervan: Grand Rapids (1982), p. 559. The writers use the example of turning a garden into a city.

4 Despite Steven's valiant—but unsuccessful—attempt to establish his incredible view!

the subjection of the ravages of sin upon the body, which degrade, humble, and destroy the body, has not yet taken place!

In 1 Corinthians 15:42 Paul writes, "The body is sown in a state of corruption; it is raised in a state of incorruption." Clearly, that which is raised is that which is sown. It is not some additional body that is substituted for the first one. What was sown? A body that was subject to corruption. What was raised? Not a substitute, but the same body that was sown.

There is a remarkable passage that helps us make the point. At the death of Jesus Christ "The graves were opened up, and many bodies of those who had fallen asleep were raised" (Matthew 27:52). Why open the graves (tombs) if *bodies* are not to issue from them? It is the physically deteriorated bodies that were "raised." What else would be raised from a burial place? What was in the grave is what came out of it, not something else. The passage plainly says that the "bodies" that were sleeping in the grave were raised. Words could hardly be clearer. How can they be interpreted to mean something else?

In John 5:28–29, similar words are used:

> *The hour is coming when all who are in the graves (literally, "tombs") will hear His voice and will come forth—those who have done good to a resurrection of life and those who have practiced evil to a resurrection of judgment.*

What is buried? The body. What arises from the grave if not the body? Surely, the only possible way of escape from that conclusion, it would seem, is to hold that it was the soul which sleeps in the ground. Yet, even that belief cannot be reasonably entertained. Who holds that the soul sleeps in tombs (*mnemeiois)*? Perhaps, with all of their other strange interpretations, there are UPs who do!

As we have seen, the UP frequently claims that promises given to readers of the biblical letters had to be fulfilled to those to whom these promises were first made, not to some later generation or to Christians in general. His argument is that it would be unreasonable to promise someone something that he will not receive in this life. That view is truly unbiblical. Listen to the writer of Hebrews:

> *These all received good testimony because of their faith; yet they didn't receive what was promised because God had something better in sight for us. So they couldn't be made perfect [complete] without us (Hebrews 11:39, 40).*

Obviously, God may make promises to those of one time that are fulfilled in a later period. Did they know that these promises were for a later time? No. Listen again to the writer of Hebrews: "These all died in faith without receiving the things that were promised" (11:13). They saw them from a "distance" and "welcomed them" (v. 13). That is as close as they got to their fulfillment—they believed God's Word though they did not receive anything tangible in this life. We, too, see the return of Jesus Christ "from a distance" when our bodies will be "conformed" to His. And we eagerly await the transformation of our bodies at His coming, though the fulfillment of this passage made in New Testament times may not happen even in our day. But should one be taught to "seek" after that which he will not receive in this life? Of course. We are taught to lay up treasures in heaven (Matthew 6:20). And these saints, to whom the promises were made, were "seeking" a heavenly homeland and city (v. 14) "that God prepared for them" (vv. 14, 16).

The transformation of our bodies at the coming of Christ and the resurrection is what is taught in the Scriptures. The identity of the body that is yet to come with the body which one now possesses is what Paul had in mind when he told Agrippa that Christ was the "first to arise from the dead" (Acts 26:23). Others, of course, had been raised by Him, but He was the "first" to be raised in a "body of glory." That he was the *first* implies that similar resurrections would follow. These passages need some thought and contemplation before we move on to others.

9

More about the Resurrection

Now, let us turn to an interesting event that is described in Acts 23 and later referred to in Acts 24:14–15. Paul was appearing before the Sanhedrin, the governing body of the people of Israel. He knew that no one from the time of Jesus' trial to that day had received a fair hearing from this religious tribunal. He was not about to be tried by people like them, so he threw the apple of discord between the members of the body who were part Pharisee and part Sadducee. Knowing that the Pharisees held to the doctrine of the resurrection of the dead while the Sadducees denied it (v. 8), he cried out in their midst, "It is about the hope and the resurrection of the dead that I am being tried" (v. 6). This caused such an uproar that it broke up the meeting, and he had to be hauled away by the Roman commander for safety's sake. Clearly, Paul was using a smart strategy to escape their condemnation. But was that all we can say about what happened? Certainly not.

In Acts 24:15 Paul explains, "I hold to a hope in God, that these men themselves accept, that there will be a resurrection of both the just and the unjust." Paul used a successful strategy, but that is not all he did; he expressed his own genuine expectation of the bodily resurrection of all men.

This was a doctrine that, he says, was held by the people of Israel as well as by the Pharisees. The way in which Luke and Paul speak of the matter makes it absolutely certain that the doctrine was firmly believed by the people—*and* it was one to which they also subscribed. The doctrinal belief was that there would be a general resurrection of all men—believers and unbelievers alike. Here is what Paul said elsewhere about the ruckus before the Sanhedrin:

> *Now I am standing trial for putting my hope in what God promised our fathers, a promise that our twelve tribes, earnestly worshiping night and day, hope to see fulfilled … Why should any of you think that it is incredible for God to raise the dead? (Acts 26:7, 8; cf. vv. 22, 23).*

Notice two things: first, that the resurrection of the dead was commonly believed by the Jews, and second, that though they looked forward to it as something they held would be fulfilled in their day, it wasn't. There was no general resurrection of the dead in 70 AD. It was not faith in the resurrection of Jesus Christ that the people expected. It was a belief in a general resurrection of all men (for confirmation of the belief among the people, see John 11:23, 24).

And when the resurrection is mentioned, it is frequently linked with Christ's bodily resurrection from the grave. We are told that, by His bodily resurrection, Christ became "the First Fruits of those who are sleeping" (1 Corinthians 15:20). That means that the resurrection of Jesus and of His people are seen as existing on the same plane. The one is the first fruits of a whole harvest of the same grain, the greater part of which remains to be harvested. The first fruits of a harvest must be of the same nature as that which follows, or they are not the first fruits of *it*. Otherwise, if first fruits, they would have to be the first fruits of something else. As His body was raised and reunited with his spirit, which had been in Paradise for three days before it was "taken up in glory" (1 Timothy 3:16), so will we be transformed and taken up with a glorified body like His in order to complete the harvest.

What do the UPs have to say about this? Noe writes, "In the middle of the 1st Century, the dead were raised."[11] Calling Jesus the First Fruits is said by UPs to mean that "a standing and full harvest is ripe and ready."[22] But there is *no point* in the text made about a harvest that is just about to take place. The time element in the passage involved has to do with order, not with proximity: it means first one thing, then later the next. That is the point of the metaphor. To sustain an unsustainable viewpoint, a sense is infused into the metaphor that was not intended. Every aspect of a metaphor must not be pursued; only that which comes from the context is legitimate.

But what of the supposed First Century resurrection? Noe continues, "Their resurrection took place in the invisible realm."[31] In other words, men will not be harvested as Jesus was![42] For Noe, the resurrection means being "raised out of Hades, the holding place of the dead."[53] Prior to Christ's resurrection, Noe believes no one had ever gone to heaven. Now the "dead in Christ" no longer go to Hades (the realm containing the spirits of the Old Testament

1 Noe, *Shattering*, p. 59.
2 Ibid., p. 62.
3 *Ibid., p*. 75.
4 And as those raised bodily from the tombs at the crucifixion.
5 *Ibid.*, p. 76.

dead).[64] They go directly to heaven. Noe claims that no one living on the earth ever heard the last trump at 70 AD; it was sounded only in Hades after Christ went and preached to those who were there.[75]

Moreover, according to Noe, the dead are raised with a "spiritual body." Indeed, he says, "The thought of a physically resurrected body is not to be found … in Scripture."[86] Is that so? Well, what of Christ's body? What of those mentioned in Matthew 27:52–53? This error he affirms, despite these physical resurrections! What, then, will this spiritual body be like?

Noe says,

> Your new spiritual body is not created from nothing, ex nihilo. But it's already being formed in your inner man.[97]

For him, that means that it is "in discontinuity with the matter composing our physical body."[108] Plainly, such a resurrection is not a resurrection from the grave, since that is where the dead *body* is. It must be a resurrection of the soul which, as we have seen according to Bray, is sleeping in the dust of the earth. He writes: "The dead who are raised come from the unseen world where they have been in sleep." In UP thought (contrary to Paul's words in Philippians 3), at the resurrection there is no transformation of the *body*;

---

6 Noe fails to tell us what happens to the dead *outside of* Christ.
7 Thus 1 Peter 3 is misunderstood. It does not teach that at His death Christ preached in Hades. What it says is that those who refused to listen to the preaching of the Spirit of Christ in Noah, as a result, are now suffering in prison. Peter makes it clear that the preaching took place while Noah was preparing the ark.
8 *Ibid.,* p. 128.
9 *Ibid.,* p. 135. What sort of body it that—a body within a body?
10 *Ibid.,* p. 136.

only a "resurrection" of something else.[111] For Bray, what is raised is the soul sleeping in the grave! For Noe, some interior life of the believer.

Christian friend, does any of this make sense? Does the UP view the resurrection as Paul did? Is the resurrected body that he looks forward to being "transformed" into a physical, glorified body like that of our risen Lord? Or is the UP concept of the resurrection some figment of the imagination designed to fit a theory?

11 Bray writes: "It is not the physical body which is raptured. It is the Christian himself who is raptured as he leaves his body behind and takes on a new body forever." *The Rapture, op. cit.*, p. 32. But leaving the body behind is not the same as having it "transformed" and "conformed." Moreover, Bray goes on to say, "Being 'caught up' does not necessarily mean the body is caught up," p. 32.

10

The General Judgment

In Chapter Four we asked why there is to be a Second Coming of Jesus Christ. The answer we gave was to bless His own by giving them a glorified body and making them His human companions forever. But there is another side of the coming that is not mentioned in 1 Thessalonians 4 or in Acts 1. It is about that I must now write. Daniel said it. In the last chapter of His book we read:

> *And many of those who sleep in the dust of the ground will awake, these to everlasting life, but the others to disgrace and everlasting contempt (Daniel 12:4, Berkeley).*

The questions arise, "About whom is Daniel speaking, and when will this resurrection of the just and the unjust take place?" Only a bit can be said about this passage because it presupposes a full knowledge of the book of Daniel. I suggest, therefore, that you read the commentary on Daniel that my colleague Milton Fisher and I wrote, *The Time of the End.*

What of Daniel 12:2? The answer to this inquiry is that God promised that persons who kept their faith or who denied it, in a time to come (after their deaths), when the results of their activities would be made known publicly, would receive their rewards of blessings or cursings. He is setting forth a general resurrection as taking place not in the intertestamental period, to which much of this portion of the book of Daniel is devoted, but in the future. Why? As an incentive for the readers to remain true during the persecution that would occur during that period of time. Those who would remain faithful could expect life everlasting in the resurrection; those who would deny their Lord would rise to everlasting damnation (here described as public disgrace and contempt).

Paul clearly referred to this same event in Acts 24:15, probably with this passage in mind when he said,

> *I hold to a hope in God, that these men themselves accept, that there will be a resurrection of both the just and the unjust.*

And,

> *He [God] declares that every human being everywhere must repent, because He has set a day in which He is going to judge the world with justice by a Man Whom He has designated to do so. And He has furnished proof of this to everybody by raising Him from the dead (Acts 17:30–31).*

In these two passages, Paul unmistakably refers to a general resurrection; that is to say, a resurrection of both the saved and the lost ("just and unjust"). As in Daniel, it is *a* (one) resurrection which includes both. And, it applies to "everybody."

Once again, in Acts 17, the resurrection is linked with Christ's resurrection: the proof of the future resurrection of men is the fact that Jesus rose from the dead. The bodily resurrection of Jesus from the grave and the resurrection of believers are in no way distinguished. Anyone reading the verse would assume (rightly) that the resurrection of Jesus and the resurrection of the dead, in general, would be resurrections of the same kind—bodily. The one is the proof of the other, in that since it happened to Jesus, we too can be certain we will also be raised. To distinguish two kinds of resurrection—one physical and the other not—is reading into the text what isn't there. It is a move of sheer desperation.

But of greater consequence to us in this chapter is the statements of Paul in regard to the judgment. He speaks of the judgment of the just and the unjust, and that Jesus is coming to judge all men everywhere. He does not say He is coming to judge Jerusalem or the Jews, but *all* are called on to repent since He will come as their judge. That runs counter to the judgment of 70 AD which was limited to the Jews.

Listen also to the Lord Jesus: "The hour is coming, and now is, when the dead will hear the voice of God's Son, and those who hear will live" (John 5:25). Unlike what Jesus will say a few verses later, this "resurrection" *is* a spiritual event—a resurrection out of spiritual death to spiritual life. Nothing is said about coming out of the grave. Those who "hear" (heed) will "live." He says nothing of a resurrection of the wicked. He is speaking only about the salvation of those who believe (cf. v. 24).

But then, in contrast, Jesus goes on to say, "the hour is coming when *all* who are in the graves [tombs] will hear His voice and will come forth—those who have done good in a resurrection of life and those who have practiced evil to a resurrection of judgment" (John 5:28, 29).

Here we have a resurrection of both the saved and the unsaved. No distinction between the resurrections of these two classes, as such, is mentioned. The distinction is in the outcome for each; their common physical, bodily resurrection will lead to eternal life or judgment.

Note, when speaking of a physical resurrection of the dead:

1. It is a general resurrection—"*all* who are in the graves will come forth."
2. It is a resurrection from the grave. The word is not sheol or Hades; it is *mnemeiois*, which means a "burial place, a tomb." Unquestionably, Jesus here refers to a physical, bodily resurrection.
3. For the unsaved, it is also a resurrection to judgment. The word "judgment" means *separation*. And at this time, when those who are in the grave shall come forth, they will be separated into two groups: those who enter into eternal life and those who are everlastingly condemned. That is exactly what Paul said when we hear him speaking in Acts 24:15—there will be a resurrection of both the just and the unjust.

As Daniel prophesied, it is one resurrection at which time all men—saved and unsaved—will be received into their eternal state. Incidentally, there is no annihilation of the lost.

In Hebrews 6:2, the author writes of the "resurrection of the dead and of eternal judgment" as two of the foundational doctrines of the faith, along with repentance, faith, etc. That resurrection is the one about which we have just been speaking; there is no reason to believe otherwise. And this very same writer explains what he means by resurrection: it is a resurrection to judgment. He writes, "Just as it is appointed for people to die only once, and after that they face judgment …" (Hebrews 9:27). Clearly, he, Jesus, and Paul all saw the judgment of men connected with the resurrection of the dead.

Furthermore, listen to Paul writing to Timothy about the One Who will "judge the living and the dead" (2 Timothy 4:1) as he declares that God will give him the "winner's wreath of righteousness lying at a distance." He further explains, "the Lord (Who is the righteous Judge) will award [the wreath] to me on that Day; and not to me alone but to *all* those who have loved His appearing" (2 Timothy 4:8–9; [italics mine]). Remember, these words were written in the context of Paul's anticipation of death (vv. 6–8). The time when He will judge and reward the living and the dead is not at Paul's death, but at "that Day" when He appears (no invisible coming here), and the dead in Christ will be raised up together with the living. This is at the time when He comes into the air and returns with His escort to the earth. The overwhelming array of Scripture heralding the coming of Jesus Christ, the resurrection of the dead from their graves, and the judgment of the just and the unjust ought to be enough to convince any unprejudiced reader that the church's doctrines, which have been held from the Reformation on, are true.

11

The Resurrection and the Last Judgment

Among the various Jewish sects, the Sadducees were the ones who denied the bodily resurrection. In Matthew 22:23ff., and Luke 20:36ff., we find Jesus answering their challenge about the seven brothers successively married to one wife. They wanted to know whose wife she would be in the resurrection. This query was probably a standard one that they used to confound the Pharisees, who did believe in the resurrection. Jesus makes it plain that there is no problem such as they envision; the only reason for their seeming dilemma, He said, is that they are ignorant of the Scriptures and the power of God (Matthew 22:29). It is clear, then, that Jesus believed in *the* "resurrection of the dead." He said nothing of any successive resurrection of the members of His church that would occur at their death or at any other time. He makes no distinction between the resurrection of Old Testament Saints and New Testament saints. From His words, no one would imagine the doctrine taught by the UPs. What He said falls entirely in line with OP teaching.

On that occasion, Jesus has some interesting things to say. He spoke of the age to come after the resurrection as a time when those who are "sons of the resurrection"[1] will neither marry nor be given in marriage. Now, if the resurrection took place in 70 AD, the following "age" (Luke 20:35), as UPs are fond of pointing out, would be the New Testament age. But, clearly, he is speaking of an age in which people will not marry, but will be like the angels. This, therefore, *must* be the age after our present age. He observes that it was not only a failure of knowledge of the Scriptures that lay behind the Sadducees' agnosticism; it was also that they had a defective view of "God's power" (Matthew 22:29). This is of significance. Many modern Sadducees who deride the idea that God could raise dead bodies out of their graves pose questions about how He could put the atoms of which their bodies were composed back together again, since their bodily elements may have become part of successive generations of those who have eaten the apple that was nourished by the decaying bodily substance in a cemetery, and so on. And they ask such questions as, "What of those who were drowned at sea, eaten by fish, and the elements of their bodies became a part of the fish's body, which, in turn, may have been caught and eaten?"—etc, etc. To all such persons (Preterists have presented this as a problem),[2] I also answer simply, "You don't know God's power!" Since Jesus thought that a sufficient answer, I do too. But we know that it is within God's power!

The return of the flesh will be important in judgment. Jesus said that God would "destroy" both the "soul and body" of some "in Gehenna." Unless the fleshly bodies of the unrighteous are raised in a form that will be subject to pain

1 Obviously, a phrase denoting that they belong to the group that attains to the resurrection of the righteous.
2 John Noe, *Left Behind*, op. cit., p. 146.

for eternity, the many passages that indicate this will take place have no referent. And, incidentally, Scripture teaches that the unsaved are raised to judgment and punishment, not to annihilation.

It would be interesting to know how UPs think it would be "more tolerable" for Tyre and Sidon "on the Judgment Day" than for people in the other cities mentioned in Matthew 12:21–23. Indeed, Jesus was the One Who said, "Let Me say something more to you: it will be more tolerable for Sodom on the Judgment Day" (v. 24). There is no doubt that Jesus looked forward to a Judgment Day in which men will be raised to judgment leading to *physical* punishment. Annihilation admits of no degrees of punishment, such as is mentioned in Luke 12:47. But if not annihilated, what happens to the risen, fleshly bodies of the wicked?

That Paul conceived of the resurrection as physical is clear from the way in which he equates our resurrection with Christ's: "He Who raised the Lord Jesus will raise us also with Jesus and will present us with you" (2 Corinthians 4:14). There is no indication that the "raising" of the believer and the "raising" of Jesus were of a different sort—one bodily, physical, the other not. Indeed, it is only fair to say that in this respect the raisings appear to be the same. Paul also speaks in Romans 8:11 of "giving life to" our "mortal bodies."[3] It is hard to gainsay that. And, in 1 Corinthians 15:52, Paul indicates that there will be a change in bodies at the resurrection. But what sort of change will that be? The "dead will be raised incorruptible." Here, once again, he speaks of the body which is now subject to corruption. Of this there can be no doubt since in the next verse he

3 The body is mortal because of Adam's sin, not because of creation.

writes of the final day: "When this corruptible [body] puts on incorruption and this mortal [body] puts on immortality." Clearly, this has not happened to the body. It is yet in the future. We know that in 1 Corinthians 15 He spoke of the physical, fleshly body because it is that alone which is "corruptible."

In 1 Corinthians 15:35–49, Paul discusses the "sort of body" with which the dead rise. He tells us that burial is like sowing a seed. When you plant wheat, you do not get barley; you get the full plant of the same grain that was planted. The seed that is sown is not the same as the plant, of course, but it is of the same character with it—it is wheat, not barley. So, too, the body that is laid aside rises again to become flesh (as Christ's did), not to become something altogether different. It is the same body, but changed. It is a body of flesh—yet glorified flesh, like our Lord's, as we have seen. Paul writes, "But God gives it the body that He wants to, and to each kind of seed its own body" (v. 38). Then he talks about different sorts of glory (vv. 40, 41) and says that the body sown in corruption rises in incorruption, and that "It is sown in a state of dishonor," but it is "raised in a state of glory" (vv. 42, 43). Note carefully that it is the same body that was sown that rises again—changed. He declares that "It is sown in a state of helplessness" and that "it is raised in a state of power" (v. 43). Throughout, he refers to the same body. What Paul is concerned to say is that the "spiritual bodies" with which the dead are raised[4] are the same bodies that once were "natural" bodies. But they have been changed. He concludes, "Just as we bore the image of the earthy man, we shall also bear the image of the heavenly

4 A spiritual body is one that is wholly under the domination of the Holy Spirit.

Man" (v. 49). Once again, the transformed bodies that we shall receive at their resurrection from the grave will be like Christ's glorified body. As John says, "We shall be like Him" (1 John 3:2). Few facts could be clearer. Yet John Noe writes, "The thought of a physically resurrected old body is not to be found here or anywhere in Scripture."[5] To the contrary, it is *precisely* that "old body," radically changed, of which Paul writes. Christ came forth from the tomb with the same, though greatly glorified, body with which He entered it. So shall we. What is sown is raised. But it will be "new," freshly remade so as to become exactly like the "glorious body of Christ."

5 John Noe, *Shattering*, op. cit., p. 128.

12

THE END OF THE WORLD

IN the UP system of things, there is no end of the world. All things[1] continue on as they are, at least so far as we know. Perhaps, the present age continues indefinitely. This idea seems to fit their theory that after 70 AD things become eternal. Men go on marrying and giving in marriage,[2] sinning, getting sick, killing one another, and dying. The idea that sin will continue, that there will be no final judgment of all men, and that God never will right all wrongs, establishing a new and different final order of things, is endemic to this dissatisfying theological system. In making the destruction of Jerusalem the fulfillment of all Old and New Testament promises, the UP has nothing to look forward to in terms of a final wrap-up of all things. Stuart says,

> Here we might pause, for Scripture prophecy guides us no further. But the close of the aeon is not the end of the world, and the fate of Israel teaches us nothing respecting the destiny of the human race.... What is to be the end and consummation of human history? Is it this earth, with

1 Op. cit., pp. 549, 550.

2 Contrary to what Christ said would happen in the age to come "when the Son of Man is revealed" (Luke 17:30). That "Day," as construed by the UP, was in 70 AD. Is there now no marrying or giving in marriage among believers?

> its precious freight of immortal and eternal interests, advancing towards light and truth, or hurrying into regions of darkness and distance from God? Where nothing has been revealed it would be the height of presumption to prognosticate the future.

John Noe speaks about "the Christian or Church age, to which there is no end."[3] In other words, nothing is prophesied about the future of the world. All prophecy was fulfilled by 70 AD. We dare not guess; we simply don't know what will happen afterward. What a dissatisfying view of the future! It is a book with no conclusion; a story without an end. This view, of course, is contrary to everything that the church has taught. And for good reasons—biblical reasons!

What does the Bible have to say about the matter? Well, to begin with, consider Peter's second letter:

> *But by the same Word, the present heavens and earth are stored up for fire, kept for Judgment Day and the destruction of ungodly men. But don't forget this one fact, dear friends, that one day with the Lord is like a thousand years, and a thousand years are like one day. The Lord is not delaying His promise in the sense that some think of delay, but He is patiently waiting for you, not wanting any of you to be destroyed, but every one to come to repentance.*
>
> *But the Lord's Day will come—as a thief—in which the heavens will pass away with a shrieking sound and the earth, and all her works, will be laid bare. Since, therefore, all these things are to be dissolved, what sort of people ought you to be in holy behavior and godliness, as you anticipate and hurry the coming of God's*

3 John Noe, *Dead in their Tracks*. IPA: Bradford (2001), p. 52.

> *Day, because of which the heavens catching fire will be dissolved and the elements burning intensely will melt? But according to His promise, we anticipate new heavens and new earth freshly made, in which righteousness will be at home (2 Peter 3:10–13).*

Now, as you read those words, do they not seem to say that there will be an end of the present world as we know it? Any reasonable person, uncommitted to a theory that he must somehow justify, would agree. But not the UPs. They must find here a reference to the destruction of Jerusalem as it introduces a new era. In order to do so, they must take all of this language figuratively, as speaking of the destruction of Jerusalem at the invisible judgment coming of Christ in 70 AD, and the state of the church after His coming. How do they do so?

Bray says,

> In actuality, this [the destruction in 70 AD] is what happened to those "elements" of the old Jewish religion—they were broken up, destroyed, loosened, and put off. This is how the elements melted in that day of the Lord when the heavens and the earth felt the judgment of God.[4]

Of course, UPs are ready with reasons for their interpretation of II Peter three. There are Old Testament passages that speak of the heavenly element being altered as a way of saying that a political or religious order of things that seemed indestructible will be destroyed and pass away. That is how Peter interpreted Joel's prophecy in Acts 2:14–21. And there are a number of other passages in the Old Testament about which the same may be said.

4 John L. Bray, *Heaven and Earth Shall Pass away.* Lakeland, n.d., p. 25.

However, the passage in 2 Peter 3 differs from them all. How? First, the passage is much longer and more detailed than any of those in the Old Testament. Second, this passage speaks about the elements of the earth and heavens burning and melting. That is new and different from any other "similar" passage. Moreover, Peter holds forth the expectation of a new heavens and earth, fashioned out of the dissolved elements of the present one, "in which righteousness will be at home" (v. 13). Certainly, that doesn't describe the world since 70 AD! And, to top it off, the comparison that is made by Peter is not between two figurative events, but between two actual ones. He says that as the world before Noah perished by the universal flood, so the world that now exists will perish by means of fire. The water and the fire are placed on the same literal level. (cf. vv. 5, 6).

And, finally, the scoffers are saying that God is delaying His promises, their argument being that "ever since the fathers fell asleep, everything remains as it was from the beginning of creation" (vv. 3, 4). Clearly, they were not talking about the fall of some old political or religious order of things—since creation, there had been innumerable such fallings. They did ignore the flood, it is true, but these other events in history to which the UPs refer were so frequent, it is not those that the scoffers could have had in mind. The fact that they speak about things not changing since the beginning of the creation adds further evidence of this fact. They are talking about something happening in the created sphere, not in the political one.

In confirmation of this teaching, it is clear from Revelation 21 and 22 that John expected the same. There, after sweeping from his day to the destruction of Satan, death, and Hades in Revelation 20 (see my book, *The Time is at Hand*, for details), he describes the final outcome of all things for the saints. To apply this to 70 AD makes no chronological sense whatever. And the description of that world to come is so magnificent that it could not refer to the church today (as some UPs think). The idea is preposterous! I am forced to conclude, therefore, that the New Testament teaches an end of the present world.

In detailing the end of the present world, Peter predicts a time of righteousness—just as John does. It is a fresh, new world of which both Apostles speak. Sin, death, pain, tears, crying, and all those things that came with the fall (even the curse itself, according to Revelation 22:3) have passed away. And we shall remember them no more. The word for "new" that both writers used is *kainos*, meaning something brand new, freshly made; not the reworking of an old politico-religious order of things. Because of all of these considerations, we should expect not a new order, but a new heavens and earth as well.

That alone is a satisfying end of all things as we now know them. God has not left us hanging in the air, wondering about the future of mankind and the final wrap-up of a sinful, cursed world. Peter writes about the emergence of a new heaven and earth after He rights all wrongs and brings about the final defeat of sin and Satan. At that time, when even "the last enemy" is defeated (surely, death has not yet been cast into the abyss!), all things will be subjected to the Father—"even the Son Himself"—so that "God will be all in all" (1 Corinthians 15:28). That time is yet in the future. On the UP view, Jesus has finished His mediatorial reign and no longer mediates for us.

Let us rejoice that our Lord Jesus has not only defeated the enemy on the cross, but that He assures us that He will come again to bring final victory to His own and final judgment to all those who oppose Him. If what we have now is the best that the earth prophesies, the Bible holds forth a rather insipid view of things.

13

Soul Sleep

SINCE we have seen that at least some UPs believe in the annihilation of the wicked (cf. Bray), and since soul sleep (at least prior to 70 AD) goes along with the teaching of annihilation, something ought to be said about these matters. Let us begin with the matter of soul sleep by citing the record of the transfiguration found in Matthew 17:1–3. The glorification of Christ on the mountain prefigured the glorified condition of the body in which He would rise and ascend to heaven in the future. Since His resurrection, He has permanently lived in a glorified body. While it is true that Enoch and Elijah did not die, but were changed (presumably as those living at the time of Christ's return will be), Moses *did* die and his body *was* buried (Deuteronomy 34:5–6). Even though he had died, on the Mount he appeared in bodily form. There is no reason to believe that Moses had been resurrected. It is more likely that, as Jesus was temporarily glorified before the time, Moses was also given a bodily form prefiguring the resurrected body he will receive. But, be that as it may, the important fact for us is that *he was alive and conscious.* He was not sleeping! This point of this passage, with reference to life after death, is not easily gainsaid by those who advocate soul sleep!

At his stoning, God granted Stephen, the first martyr, a vision of Jesus sitting on the right hand of God. Accordingly, as Jesus' words on the cross indicate, upon death God would receive his spirit. Stephen's prayer echoed His Lord's words (see Acts 7:59; Luke 23:46). Obviously, Stephen's request to Christ was at death to take him in the form of a spirit separated from its body into His presence. His body was buried, but *He* did not descend into the grave; His body did, but He went to heaven. Death, then, is the separation of the spirit from the body. That fact James makes perfectly clear: "Just as the body without the spirit is dead, so also faith without works is dead." (James 2:26). The application James makes is based upon the belief that the spirit leaves the body at death. That James could make his argument about works and faith attests to the solidly recognized fact that the Scriptures teach the separation of body and soul at death.

The body is buried. Since the spirit is separated from the body, it is not buried. It is the body that everywhere is said to sleep; not the soul (cf., for example, 1 Corinthians 15:35). God created Adam by forming a lifeless body and then animated it by breathing into it the breath of life. At death, the separation between the spirit and body that existed before God's breath animated Adam once more takes place. At the resurrection, the two will once more be united. Man's natural state clearly is a union of body and soul; however, sin brought about a separation of the two. But was the animating breath of God a dead, unconscious thing? Hardly. It was the very thing that gave life to Adam. Doubtless, that is why it was called the "breath of *life*" (Berkeley). Listen to this: "The Lord God formed man from the dust of the ground, and breathed into his nostrils the breath of life; and man became a living soul" (Genesis 2:7). The animating breath of God, from which man's soul was derived, was itself what gave man life and consciousness. How, then, could it be unconscious or non-existent during the intermediate state? If one says that spirit merely meant earthly, physical "life," he must remember those passages just quoted in which our Lord and Stephen spoke of their spirits going to God. To commend one's spirit "into God's hands," and to ask Jesus to "receive one's spirit" is very different from suddenly becoming unconscious.

The concept of Paradise ("park")[1] is used as an alternate term for heaven. The thief on the cross was told by Christ that he would be in Paradise with Him that very day (Luke 23:43). It was his spirit that went there. How do we know that? From Paul's certain designation of it in 2 Corinthians 12:2, 4 where he speaks of being "snatched away to the third heaven." He also describes the event as being "snatched away into Paradise." It is plain that he equated the two. And, notice the terminology: he was "snatched away." To where? Heaven. In complete harmony with this are Paul's statements in 2 Corinthians 5:6, 8: "while we are at home in the body, we are away from the Lord"; "we would prefer to leave the body and go home to be with the Lord." Could any statement be plainer? In leaving the body, Paul (and those Christians for whom he speaks when using the word "we") expected to be with the Lord—not unconsciously lying in the grave together with his body. And notice the *way* in which he speaks; the disembodied spirit has full personality: he identifies himself with it. It was *he* who was snatched away to Paradise and heard things not lawful for him to

1 The "Garden of Eden" means "The park of pleasures."

utter. How could that happen if he were detached from the body in soul sleep? He was conscious all the time. His words make it clear that Paul believed one could consciously exist in Paradise without his body.

In Luke 20:37–38, we have additional information in the account of the Lord Jesus' encounter with the Sadducees. He refers to the Old Testament, by which He proves that there was conscious life after death. Since God called Himself "the God of Abraham, the God of Isaac and the God of Jacob," He pointed out, they "are all alive" (v. 38). How is that? Because, as He said, "God is not the God of the dead, but of the living." Were they not dead then? Of course they were. Their bodies were buried in the ground. But they—their conscious personalities—were still alive. Their *spirits* survived death. They were not subject to death. He could have been referring to nothing else.

Consider Romans 8:38–39. Paul writes:

> *I am convinced that neither death nor life, nor angels, nor rulers, nor things present, nor things to come, nor powers, nor height nor depth, nor anything else in creation can separate us from God's love in Christ Jesus our Lord.*

It seems clear from these words that Paul considered his soul (and the souls of other Christians) immune from the effects of death and things to come. But it is true that he died, and very difficult things did come his way. What did he mean by those words? He meant that his bond with Christ was so certain that nothing could keep him from being with Him and enjoying His love, and, he said, that even included death. Again, we see Paul thinking of himself apart from the body, which he would leave behind at death and which would be separated from Christ. To enjoy His "love" after death, he would have to remain a conscious spirit. That this is what he had in mind is confirmed by his words in 1 Thessalonians 5:10, "so that whether we awake or asleep we may live together with Him." Whether he was alive in body and soul or whether his body slept and his spirit alone remained alive, either way—in the body or out of it—Paul as a person would "live" with Christ. And in Philippians 1:23, Paul spoke of his "desire to depart and be with Christ (which is far better)." Note once more, he, the essential person, would "be with Christ" at death.

I could go on to mention the "spirits of just men made perfect" in the Jerusalem which is above (Hebrews 12:22–24); John 17:24 where Jesus prays that those the Father gave Him would be where He is "that they may see" His "glory," and of passages like Luke 16:23, 25 in the account of the rich man and Lazarus whose persons were alive after the death of the body in joy and in suffering.[2] But it is unnecessary to do so. That which has already been set forth is sufficient to make the point: the spirit remains conscious, alive, after the death of the body. Soul sleep is simply not a biblical option.

2 Many have observed that this is not a parable because in parables persons are not named. But even if it were a parable, doesn't it teach conscious existence after death?

14

The End of the Line for the Lost?

THAT'S what the annihilationists believe. John Bray, an Unorthodox Preterist, is one of them. It is sad to say that he thinks that this is so, in spite of all of the contrary evidence found in the Scriptures. Nevertheless, in an article entitled "The Meaning of the Word Perish," when speaking of the word "perish," here is what he wrote:

> It goes without saying that the word does **not** mean to be consciously tormented[1] forever and forever ... The Bible nowhere declares that a soul (or a body or a spirit) will be consciously tormented forever in Hell. If there is such a passage, let someone find it.

The challenge can be met. There is not only one passage; there are many. So it goes without saying that Bray's assertion does *not* go without saying.

First, let's get some things straight. There are few who openly profess to believe in "annihilationism." Usually, they call the belief the Doctrine of Conditional Immortality. I suppose it sounds better! They affirm that man was born

1 It means "ruined"; it does not mean to go out of existence.

mortal, not immortal, and that only those who are saved thereby acquire immortality. All others simply do not participate in ongoing life of any kind beyond death. There are varieties on the theme; however, some think that the Lord will raise the lost, judge them, and then sentence them to non-existence. But, by far, most think that there simply is no hope for them after death. Like the animals, once they die, that's it!

As Bray says, the lost will not suffer for their sins in hell. A few believe that they will rise and suffer for a time and then go into non-existence. Some think that their souls are raised at the resurrection for *judgment*—in which the sentence given is annihilation. Now, it is difficult to determine whether or not a UP believes in annihilationism. Many of the UPs that I have read do not accept the doctrine in any form. They have their own peculiar twist(s) on the resurrection of the dead and the judgment.

Apparently, John Noe, a prominent member of The International Preterist Association from whom I have quoted frequently, holds to the doctrine of Conditional Immortality. He writes, "Some, your author included, feel Adam and Eve were created mortal."[2] That is to say, if God were not to give men life through Christ, none would live eternally. He thinks that, possibly, Adam and Eve would have become immortal had they eaten of the tree of life. He says that we cannot "regain in Christ what was not lost in Adam."[3] He

2 *Shattering, op. cit.*, p. 43. One cannot help wondering whether this means that Jesus Christ, Who was a true man, was also born mortal! Think of the consequence of such a view. It would mean either that He bore our sins throughout His lifetime or that the "wages of sin" is *not* "death." The view throws doubt upon Jesus' substitutionary death for sinners *on the cross*.

3 *Ibid.*, p. 48. What he has in mind is immortality.

claims that what was lost in the garden was not immortality; it was the *possibility* of it. That means that those who are "in Christ" only regain access to the tree of life. Does he hold that all will eat—or could some fail to do so in eternity? While in this book he doesn't say so, the logical consequence of his view of Conditional Immortality is that the wicked, who are not in Christ, are not raised.

Frost has the view that what is called the 70 AD "resurrection" included "the Old Testament saints as well as the unrighteous." Those "'unrighteous' were thrown into the lake of burning sulphur."[4] But he does not tell us the ultimate destiny of those who are thrown into the lake of fire. There are two possibilities: the orthodox view—they will be in torment everlastingly—or the unorthodox view—they were annihilated by this fire or burned for a time and then annihilated. It is unclear from his interesting and otherwise informative book what Frost's view of the destiny of the unsaved may be.

Now the problem is that, in the UP books that I have read, very little (if anything) is said about the resurrection of the wicked dead. Almost all of the discussion has to do with the resurrection and eternal state of the righteous. Bray, as we saw, is an exception; he is quite clear about his annihilationist view. Others are not so forthcoming. It is difficult to discover what UPs believe about this all-important matter. It seems that their beliefs are not monolithic. One can only wonder whether this glaring omission is that because they believe in annihilationism of one sort or another, and are reticent to admit the fact. I raise the question of the state of the wicked at death and afterward, since it is possible that

4 Samuel Frost, *The Millennial Post*, Vol. 1, Issue 5, Orlando: 2002, p. 2.

you may encounter a UP who holds to the Conditional Immortality doctrine. In such a case, you will not be shocked, but (rather) prepared for the encounter.

What is the orthodox belief, and what does the Bible tell us? Perhaps John Calvin spelled out the orthodox view as clearly as any when he wrote,

> The immortality of the soul, which we assert, and which we say consists in a perception of good and evil, exists even when it is dead, and [we hold] that death is something else than the annihilation to which they would reduce it.[5]

This is the belief that the Protestant church has held ever since the Reformation. To deny the conscious existence in which a person (out of his body) is capable of distinguishing good from evil is clearly unorthodox, as is the annihilation of his soul and body.

It is interesting to ask UPs a question of this sort: "Given the understanding of the resurrection as an event in which one immediately enters heaven, just what sort of resurrection of the wicked do you believe in?" Surely it cannot be that the wicked enter heaven with the righteous. In the light of Daniel 12:2, in which he speaks of both the just and the unjust who "sleep in the dust of the ground" awakening, some to joy and the rest to disgrace and contempt, it seems fair to pose the above question. Daniel's general resurrection of both those who are saved and those who are not allows for no separate resurrections. Both sorts of persons, whose

5 John Calvin, "Psychopannychia" in *Tracts and Treatises, Vol. 3*. Eerdmans: Grand Rapids (1958), p. 453. The title of the treatise which he wrote means "awake through the whole night" and was his first theological publication.

bodies are asleep in the ground, will be awakened (or re-animated), in a new form, by union with their spirits. I'd like to know how those who believe in soul sleep handle the problem.

Stevens, president of the IPA, has abandoned what he calls the "process" view, which holds that there will be progressive individual resurrections at the death of each person. Instead, he now thinks that there was a "tangible" resurrection in 70 AD. He teaches that those believers who were alive at that time, along with those who are raised from Hades, were caught up by Christ in a "rapture." He does not, however, think that the "decomposed bodies" of men will be raised. Obviously, he too speaks only of the righteous dead, not of the wicked. Were the lost given new bodies at that time? Did God create *perfect* new bodies? Since He creates nothing that is imperfect, we cannot abide such a thought. Were these new bodies then cast into hell? Or were they annihilated? It is clear that the wicked will be judged, so they cannot merely be left in the grave with their souls sleeping. Are they given immortality in order to suffer everlastingly, even though that is said to be possessed only by those who are in Christ? Clearly, the problem is a vexing one for the UP. The only way out of the dilemma, it seems, is that in 70 AD the bodies of the wicked were raised in some sense as some sort of new entities and then annihilated. I cannot say what Stevens holds about this matter, since, as I said, the books of his that I have read are silent about it. The UPs have many ingenious ways of "supporting" their beliefs, so I wouldn't be surprised if they were able to come up with another unique twist.

The Bible teaches the eternal punishment of the lost. Bray is wrong. *All* of those bodies sleeping in the dust of the ground, about which Daniel wrote, will be raised to judgment. If the wicked person does not have a conscious existence, how then can he be judged? There are consequences of the judgment that only a conscious person can bear (disgrace and everlasting contempt as Daniel 12:2 declares). How can one who is raised to disgrace and (note) *everlasting* contempt be thus disgraced if annihilated? There can be no doubt that what is "raised" from the dust of the ground is the *body*, which (to the contrary) Stevens thinks will remain in a decomposed condition. As we have seen, it is bodies that are buried in the dust of the ground, not souls! Can he really believe that what are deposited in the ground are souls that will awake to judgment? That is a hard pill to swallow—I would think even too large for most UPs!

If the soul is naturally mortal and receives immortality only by trusting in Christ and being allowed to eat of the tree of life, how can the *wicked* be raised at all? Are they recreated? Will they become immortal in order to suffer everlastingly? The question is left unanswered. Is that because the UPs have no answer?

There are many biblical proofs of the conscious existence of the soul after death. One such interesting incident, which refutes the doctrine of annihilationism, is found in the story of the witch (medium) at Endor recorded in 1 Samuel 28. That the Jews believed in necromancy (contacting the dead) is clear. Otherwise, the practice would not have been forbidden (see Deuteronomy 18:10–12). The "witch," whose practice was fraudulent,[6] was utterly shocked when Samuel actually appeared (v. 11). She didn't expect it, but he did. Note, Samuel—who had died and was buried—was

6 The Hebrew gives reason to believe that she was a ventriloquist.

consciously alive! Like Elijah and Moses on the Mount of Transfiguration, was he given a temporary body?

I am not going to take the time to rehash the abundant evidence for a conscious existence of the soul after death. There are an adequate number of reference works that do so. My purpose is to show, biblically, that in the *eternal state,* the lost will consciously suffer in hell. And, I will not take a great deal of time doing that either, since the issue is adequately handled in the standard texts. I shall mention, then, only two passages that powerfully relate to the question. The first is Jude 7:

> *In the same way, Sodom and Gomorrah and the cities around them, that in a similar manner engaged in sexual immorality and went away after different flesh, are set forth as an example of suffering the punishment of eternal fire.*

First, it is important to understand that Jude believed the angels were "awaiting the judgment of the Great Day" (v. 6). So too, "in a similar manner," the wicked about whom Jude speaks would be kept for the Day of judgment. Second, Jude taught that they will receive the "punishment" of eternal fire. Like it or not, the passage clearly indicates that they will suffer eternally. Third, the punishment (*dike* in the original, which means "judicial sentence, penalty") that is meted out to them at the judgment of the Great Day is plainly one that indicates the utmost suffering. The larger point to understand, however, is that what happened to Sodom as the fire from heaven fell, is an "example" of the suffering that the wicked men mentioned by Jude will endure. It will be eternal. In addition, in verse 13, Jude tells us that they are like "wandering stars for whom the dark gloom has been reserved forever" (cf. 2 Peter 2:17). Undoubtedly, that is an additional reference to the eternal punishment of the wicked under a second figure of speech—eternal gloom. As the angels, chained in gloomy darkness for a time, await the Day of Judgment (v. 6), so too, these men await the sentence of *eternal* gloom and *eternal* fire. Words could hardly be plainer. The wicked will be judged and sentenced to eternal punishment in which they will *suffer*.

A second passage that teaches the eternal punishment of the wicked is Matthew 10:28:

> *Don't be afraid of those who kill the body but can't kill the soul; rather, be afraid of the One Who can destroy both soul and body in Gehenna.*

This fearful warning tells us several things. First, the soul cannot be killed by putting someone to death. Therefore, to speak of the soul as "dead" is wrong. Second, God will destroy some in Gehenna (in the place of eternal fire; see Mark 9:47, 49). Gehenna is a place of punishment—not annihilation—as is indicated in the passage from Mark just cited. Jesus removes any doubt about the matter. Referring to the trash dump outside of Jerusalem called Gehenna (getting its name from "the Valley of Hinnom" where in order to consume the garbage, fires burned and maggots feasted), He makes an interesting comparison. In the earthly Gehenna, the fires were sometimes extinguished; in the eternal Gehenna of punishment, they would never cease burning. The same is said to be true of the worms (or maggots) that were ever present to feed on the garbage; they died, but the punishment men would receive would be like worms eternally eating away at them. Obviously, there is no reference to some *temporary* suffering in these words. In contrast to conditions in the earthly dump, where fire and worm were not eternal, the future Gehenna into which the wicked are to be cast is. That is not annihilation. Bray wanted a verse; I have gone the second mile and given him two!

Finally, the passage teaches that both the body and the soul of the wicked could be cast into the eternal Gehenna. In addition to disproving annihilationism, let me ask how that can take place on a UP interpretation of the text? How can the bodies of the wicked be cast into Gehenna eternally? If their first bodies decomposed never to be raised again, with what sort of bodies do *they* arise? Does God give them new bodies in which to suffer? All of these matters—and more—clearly require a view that is contrary to annihilationism.

Conclusion

To some, the discussions in this book may have seemed either esoteric or unimportant. That is because they have never encountered a Preterist—of any sort! Let me assure you that an understanding of matters that I have raised may be vitally important to you in the days ahead. Not only will you eventually be confronted by those who teach Preterism, but for the sake of a loved one, you may be challenged to refute them. In my opinion, to be uninformed concerning these issues is a great mistake. Unorthodox Preterism is coming on hard. And its proponents are inveterate proselytizers. Pastor, elder, interested Christian, for once, why not become informed beforehand rather than wait until your congregation is adversely affected?

As I have told you, I am a Preterist of the OP camp. As this book indicates in no uncertain terms, I consider UP Preterism to be seriously in error. In order to obtain a knowledge of Preterism of the orthodox type, you may read several of my books in which the view is set forth. In particular, I would suggest *The Time is at Hand, Signs and Wonders in the Last Days,* and *The Time of the End: Daniel Reclaimed.*

If you don't know "what the fuss is all about," remember what I said at the beginning of the book: three major doctrines of our faith have been denied (or, at best, grossly misunderstood and misstated) by the UPs. This attack upon the orthodox doctrines of the Second Coming, the Resurrection of the Body, and the Judgment of all men can only lead people astray. Already, it has had the effect of driving John Bray (and who knows how many others who don't write about it) into a denial of eternal punishment. Moreover, as you probably gathered in the discussion, it would seem that the most logical conclusion that a UP would have to reach is "soul sleep" prior to the resurrection.[1] How else could he avoid this implication of UPism? If it is the body that is not "sleeping" (as several passages indicate), but decomposing so as never to rise again, then what is? All that is left is the spirit or soul!

I want to reiterate that OPs believe in the three doctrines which are denied (or so altered that they ought no longer be considered under those headings) by UPs, namely the resurrection of dead bodies from the grave, the Second Coming as an event that has not yet occurred but that will take place some time in the future, and the General judgment of both the just and the unjust at the resurrection. OPs agree with the UPs that a number of passages that have often been applied to the future ought to be understood as referring to the Judgment Coming of 70 AD. They do believe that all of those things that were predicted to come upon the generation alive in Christ's day, did come. But, unlike the UPs, they do not relegate the fulfillment of *all* prophecy to the destruction of Jerusalem, which occurred in the year 70 AD.

So, while warning you to beware of the doctrines set forth by UPs, I think you would be wise to investigate the teachings of Ops. You owe it to yourself to become familiar

1 A conundrum: what good would Christ do by preaching to the sleeping dead in Hades?

with them since I predict you will also hear more and more about their teachings. Men like R. C. Sproul have adopted the OP position. That fact, in itself, ought to spur you to do such a study. A student of the Bible who is concerned with truth must not allow himself to ignore views different from his own. At a minimum, he should learn and understand them even if he does not accept them. That is how I became familiar with the UP position. Because the proponents of the UP viewpoint had so many correct and interesting exegetical ideas, I was attracted to their system. It fascinated me. But once I had delved into it in greater depth (I have not read all of their writings, however), I soon learned what was wrong. Then, the fascination grew thin and, finally, disappeared altogether.

In framing a reply to various aspects of the UP system, not only was I able to recognize their errors, but, in addition, my own viewpoint was greatly strengthened. I was able to reconfirm the fact that Preterism of the OP sort held up while that of the UPs did not. And in perusing UP materials, I was helped to sharpen my understanding of some things that before were somewhat vague to me.

So I call upon you to be a Berean. Seek to know whether the things that others teach (including what I have written) are true. Note particularly that when Paul commends the Bereans for their diligence in seeking truth, he does not commend them for seeking error. There is a difference. The former are interested in learning God's will; the latter may not be. Errors will emerge during an honest search. Therefore, let me urge you to search the Scriptures daily to see if the things discussed in this book are *true*.

I hope that as you begin, you will be stimulated by what you read to complete the search. "But," you say, "anyone who has read thus far must have completed it." No, that isn't what I mean. Some people read the conclusion to a book in order to decide whether to read the whole book or not. That is one problem. But a far greater problem is when a person reads merely out of curiosity, but not to discover truth. All such, instead, should learn to read in order to determine what God has taught about those matters considered in this book. And in order to do so (as the Bereans did), they must read with their Bibles open to the pertinent passages, taking nothing for granted. Consulting a number of good commentaries and reference volumes would also be of help. But of greatest importance, sincerely ask God to enable you by His Spirit to understand the Scriptures as you study. Be a Berean!

For a complete list of all Jay Adams' titles published by the Institute for Nouthetic Studies, scan this QR code. It will take you to our online bookstore.

www.ingramcontent.com/pod-product-compliance
Lightning Source LLC
LaVergne TN
LVHW010938110826
845149LV00013B/2662

* 9 7 8 1 9 7 0 4 4 5 3 1 2 *